DATA LEADERSHIP

Stop Talking About Data and Start Making an Impact!

by Anthony J. Algmin

DATAVERSITY Press

DATAVERSITY Education, LLC

DATAVERSITY Press

A division of DATAVERSITY Education, LLC

ISBN 978-0-578-54270-6

This publication contains the opinions and ideas of its authors. It is intended to provide helpful and informative material on the subject matter covered. It is sold with the understanding that neither the authors nor the publisher are engaged in rendering legal or other professional services. If legal advice or other expert assistance is required, the services of a professional person should be sought.

All DATAVERSITY books are available at a special quantity discounts to use as premiums and sales promotions, or for educational use. Special books, or book excerpts, can also be created to fit specific needs.

For more information write: DATAVERSITY Press, 13020 Dickens Street, Studio City, California, 91604, USA

For all who do what they do so I can do this.

ACKNOWLEDGMENTS

Thank you, as sincerely and gratefully as I'm capable of communicating:

First to Tony Shaw and the entire DATAVERSITY® team, as we have been through so much together over the last many years. Shannon Kempe, Cristina Lim, Charles Roe, this couldn't have been the same without your influence. Thank you for taking a chance on me.

To Danette McGilvray, who has been there for me with unwavering support and guidance for years. Your contributions to this book have been substantial, and I can't thank you enough for carving out the time to provide detailed feedback.

To the Data Management thought-leaders who have welcomed me as a peer, and provided the support and guidance necessary to help bring this work to fruition: Davida Berger, Kelle O'Neal, Malcolm Chisholm, John Ladley, Anne Buff, Peter Aiken, Len Silverston, William Tanenbaum, April Reeve, Frank Cerwin, Theodore Hills, Catherine Nolan, Thomas Redman, Gene Boomer, Mike Bowers, Michele Koch, Barbara Deemer, Sue Geuens, Sunil Soares, Stan Christiaens, John Zachman, Michael Miller, Jonathan Adams, and Melanie Mecca.

To my family, who has been patient and supportive throughout the many hours this endeavor has taken me away from you.

To those that gave me the career experiences to write this book: Morningstar, Stein Roe Investment Counsel, REFCO, Ronin Capital, West Monroe Partners, Chicago Transit Authority, Uturn Data Solutions, and all of the colleagues and clients I've had the honor to work alongside throughout my journey. Many of us are still close, but others will never realize how much our time together has meant to me.

And last but not least, to two of my closest mentors and friends, without whom I may not have found my way in this space: Kasu Sista and Bob Seiner. You are both passionate and wise, demanding and forgiving, inspiring and frustrating, and have each pushed me to become my best, professionally and personally. I cannot possibly thank you enough, so I'll pay it forward whenever I can. I'm sure you'd do the same in my shoes—because you have.

FOREWORD

It is both a privilege and an honor to provide a foreword for my friend Anthony Algmin's new book on Data Leadership. I was first exposed to him at a conference almost a decade ago. I sat in on one of his presentations at a DATAVERSITY event and left the session feeling inspired by the passionate messages Anthony shared as a former Chief Data Officer of Chicago Transit Authority. I knew immediately that I had met a data soulmate.

Over the years, Anthony and I have had many deep conversations about the direction of the Data Management industry and the leadership required to effect change. The essence of this book represents his Data Leadership Framework and many of his most practical and pragmatic thoughts and beliefs about what is necessary to be a successful Data Leader.

When Anthony first introduced me to his idea of writing a book, he told me that he wanted to write "The Book on Data Leadership"—which we both thought was a brilliant title. Shortened to "Data Leadership" with the subtitle "Stop Talking About Data and Start Making an Impact!," this book is a call to action for people who strive to be Data Leaders. Anthony's regular column in my publication, "The Data Administration Newsletter" (TDAN.com), is called "Make An Impact," and that name perfectly describes his goal for this book.

Anthony and I share in many activities and both have a strong relationship with DATA-VERSITY Education, LLC. I have entertained Anthony as a guest on several episodes of my DATAVERSITY webinar series. This book represents DATAVERSITY's first foray into book publishing, and they couldn't have picked a better person and topic to venture down that path.

Across the history of the Data Management industry, there have been many people who have been data thought-leaders. The role models I looked up to when I was getting started were Larry English, John Zachman, Clive Finkelstein, Barb von Halle, and Bill Inmon. Along the way, there were too many others to name here, but these are the people who I held in seriously high regard. I wanted, in many ways, to be a Data Leader just like them.

Anthony has shared with me often that he now views me in the same light I viewed my role models in, and I am humbled by comments like these. I never expected to have people look up to me the way that I looked up to the Data Leaders that I mentioned. If you are looking for people to look up to in the Data Management industry, start with somebody like Anthony Algmin and you will head down a favorable and influential path.

With people like Anthony Algmin, the Data Management and Data Leadership industries are in excellent hands, boding well for the future.

Robert S. (Bob) Seiner

INTRODUCTION

Data today is a study of contrasts.

On one extreme, we have the most innovative companies doing unbelievable things with data and analytics—like when SpaceX successfully launched a rocket into space, and then used real-time analytics to control and safely land an unmanned booster rocket upright on a barge floating in the ocean. Seeing a video of the landing for the first time, the most rational response a person can have is, "Those special effects look totally fake."

But they aren't special effects at all—it actually happened! And now, rockets are landing backwards all over the place like it's no big deal. Cars are logging millions of autonomous miles, we talk to our TVs, and everybody carries a device in their pocket that can instantly connect us to the answer to nearly any question we can imagine. And that last one has been the case for over a decade!

All of these things are amazing, every single day. It is an incredible time to be alive, and we should all be walking around astonished by what surrounds us, and in awe of what awaits us on the horizon.

Instead, our expectations have risen with these capabilities, and we tend to have diminished tolerance for failures to meet these higher standards. If Netflix buffers for 20 seconds on our 65" TV, we call it a piece of junk, or if we request a password reset email and it doesn't immediately hit our inbox, we assume they have been hacked and we start making plans to cancel our account and move to a competitor.

In our personal lives, we have such constantly profound data-driven experiences that it is especially frustrating in our work lives when we can't even get the numbers on two reports to match! How is it that we can go from literally talking to our entertainment devices at home to feeling like we are back in the dark ages of the 1990s when we head to work?

It used to be that we went to work to access the good stuff. The technology capabilities at the office were far superior to those that individuals could own, mostly because the costs of high technology were out of the reach of individual consumers. Only businesses with big checkbooks could afford the big servers and the software applications to run on them.

Sure, businesses today still have the big checkbooks and an ability to buy fancy technologies far beyond our consumer-grade phones. And clearly some, like the backwards-rocket-landing ones, are putting that technology to productive use. Then why do so many of our companies have such difficulty with something as simple as basic reporting?

It's because this is not a technology issue at all. Though Data Analytics almost always *involves* technology, it is not fundamentally *about* technology. Data is the result of our best attempts to record truths related to our businesses. Data Analytics then evaluates and applies these truths to influence business activities so that future truths will hopefully improve by comparison.

Put more simply: data informs us about our businesses, and then we can either use that knowledge to improve what we do, or decide that change is hard and go back to punching the clock, blindly hoping what we've always done will keep working.

Sometimes I wonder if organizations are even serious about competing. We see incredible innovation happening around us, but most of our organizations have failed to fully capitalize on the power contained in our data. We create pretty visualizations to obscure the unreliability of our data, and when we do luck into real data-driven insights, we ignore them and make decisions based on emotion or gut-instinct.

MAKE-AN-IMPACT! Data is quickly becoming our most abundant resource, while simultaneously propelling us to new heights in our ability to squander valuable things.

Our organizations currently find themselves largely incapable of harnessing the riches that data can provide. Instead we find ourselves at greater risk, fearing data breaches and privacy violations that make the evening news and the trending topics on Twitter. It is not that we think data is worthless—far from it! The executives I encounter almost universally see the potential value in data, but struggle with knowing what to do about it.

It's as if you put me in the world's best diamond mine: there is a small chance I might get something valuable out of the ground, but there is near-certainty that I would hurt myself. Getting value from data is probably a lot like diamond mining. I personally know very little about diamond mining, but what I suspect is that it is highly complex, requires a significant investment to do well, and results in incredible financial returns when done right. If that hypothesis holds true, data and diamonds have a whole lot in common.

Data is complex, just like the truths it attempts to describe. There are different perspectives, and it may not always be easy to identify which of those perspectives are correct in which circumstances. The systems and processes to record and relay data must serve many different purposes, and have significant technology and business considerations and implications. Though the complexity is palpable (especially at large scale), if we can break it down into smaller, more actionable chunks, we will find data excellence is within our reach. That is why we are here.

Data Leadership is achieved by optimally applying our energies across Data Management functions to maximize business outcomes for our organizations. Data Leadership gives us the ability to turn what feels like an impossible challenge into an engine of data-driven business improvement. We carve up the complexity of all the things we must do to transform any organization from do-the-same-thing-and-hope-for-the-best into one that makes the most of its data potential. Everything we talk about in this book centers around using the data to create something of value. This we will conveniently refer to as Data Value.

  MAKE-AN-IMPACT! Maximizing Data Value is the most important thing.

Fortunately for those interested in getting incredible value from data, you are in the right place! Add into that the fact that in the next few years any organization that does not become fundamentally data-driven will inevitably be destroyed by their competition, whether current adversaries or new disruptors.

I once had an employer tell me I couldn't put a statement like that into a white paper because it was too provocative. I countered with, "But it is true, and also incredibly important. Shouldn't we share this with people?" Long story short, I don't work there anymore. Never be afraid to speak the truth just because someone might be uncomfortable with the consequences.

Becoming proficient at turning data into improved business outcomes is now required for any organization. The competitive advantages gained by establishing deep and detailed understanding of today's truths will uncover countless opportunities otherwise hidden from our view. If we do not, our competitors will, and they are probably already ahead in the journey. So everybody should be here with us—and discounted bulk orders of this book are available direct from the publisher!

What is scarier than the fact that data excellence is now necessary (not just helpful) is that the bar of reasonable competence is moving so high, so fast, that I fear many of our existing organizations will simply disappear rather than adapt quickly and remain competitive.

In my home suburb in Chicago, they tore down the long-shuttered Kmart to make way for a Mariano's grocery store. The Dominick's grocery down the street had shut down a couple years earlier after succumbing to competitive pressures chain-wide. It now sits empty. So one fast-growing grocery store brand replaced a dying one a half-mile away, and was built on a property that used to house one of the failed precursors to Walmart and Amazon. These are big businesses getting thrashed by one-time up-and-comers like Whole Foods and Trader Joe's. Grocery stores! Classic examples of old school, low-margin businesses being disrupted by newcomers willing to take chances based on data.

If we think data-driven strategy and operational efficiencies are not being leveraged by the upstarts in our own industries, then we are missing everything. If we want our organizations to remain relevant, we must maximize the use of data to get better at what we do best.

The opportunity to deliver on the promise of data to our organizations is beckoning. Consider recent history and where it's all heading from here. Looking back at pictures from the 1990s, you might think, "That's so cute!" Things were so much simpler then, with our enormous computers and phones with cords. We had predictions what the future would hold, but overemphasized physical innovations like flying cars over the impact of the internet and supercomputers in every pocket. We are now in the middle of something big, with a front-row seat to watch history repeat itself!

Today we are far beyond where we were, but nowhere near where we are going. Tremendous changes are happening with data and technology. We are transforming from batch processing to continuous availability and reliance on constant uptime. We once had to go sit at a desk to amplify our capabilities with computers, then one day laptops let us work from the couch, and eventually mobile devices allowed for instant-access wherever we want it. Evolving rapidly now, the Internet of Things (IoT) will have us living with an array of connected devices that are always on, always monitoring, and hopefully always improving our lives.

Everything is trending smaller, faster, and more connected—to the point that physical hardware endpoints are often being reduced to their pure physical role. From RFID chips to beacons to fitness watches—by offloading the complex data processing, networks of cheap, independent sensors can become ubiquitous.

The stakes couldn't be higher than they are with data. Why have we not fixed this by now? It's not like data wasn't around 20 or 30 years ago. It almost feels like we are honoring some silly tradition mandating that we stink at Data Management—but the pain is getting far worse because the pace of data growth, along with the technology capabilities that supercharge it, are increasing exponentially in their power. The gap between the exceptional data-driven organizations and the marginal ones is also ever-increasing, and we are seeing the consequences everywhere we look, even with our hometown grocery stores.

We pay so much attention to data and technology that we may be inclined to think that data and technology is where we will find the solution to the problem. I believe this is wrong. The answers to realizing the value of data are actually found within the people and organizational dynamics of our companies. This book explains why this is the case, and helps us understand what we need to do to overcome these challenges—and create the data-driven organizations that will succeed in the coming years.

By studying the lessons in this book, you will learn how to maximize the value of data. You will see how it all fits together and will change the future of your organization. Whether you are an executive, sales rep, department head, copy editor, data scientist, or DBA, this book is for you. It does not matter your role, just that you think data might help in some way.

Data Value is the common thread, and it is up to those of us who see its potential to take action to make it real. After all, the folks who do not yet see the value in data will not be the ones to pave the way.

MAKE-AN-IMPACT! The magic is in balancing all of the drivers of potential value, putting them all together in a harmonious way to realize the most Data Value.

If this all seems a little strange or esoteric, don't worry. This whole introduction is like a data-flavored amuse-bouche (and if you needed to look that up, that makes two of us!). We will cover Data Value so much throughout this book that it will become second nature to you by the time you are done reading (or listening, if you've chosen the audiobook option with my lush baritone vocals).

And I guess now is as good a time as any to address my writing style—some may call it "informal" whereas others, like my seventh-grade teacher (Mrs. Nelson), would probably say the style is "linguistically a poor choice for the topic of discussion." I like to think of it as a little more approachable than your typical Data Management or business book, but mostly I needed to keep us both awake while exploring subjects that can be a bit on the dry side. This does not mean I'm any less (or more) qualified, knowledgeable, or passionate about Data Leadership than if I wrote the way my public school education taught me—it's just that I'm trying to make fifty-something thousand words of Data Management and organizational theory a little more tolerable for all of us. And isn't that the most important thing?

No, maximizing Data Value is the most important thing. Have you not been paying attention so far?

And Data Leadership is how we do it—we're going to change the world with this stuff!

PART 1: DATA LEADERSHIP FOUNDATIONS

1 THE VALUE OF DATA

Data Leadership is defined as how we choose to apply our limited energy and resources toward creating data capabilities to influence our business. There are so many options for how these energies may be applied, and breaking them down and understanding when and how to apply them is the focus of much of the book. I'm not going to claim it's easy, but at least Data Leadership activities can be directly controlled.

To make it more tangible, think of Data Leadership as the factory where we build the data sprockets and widgets that our customers will use. We may create data capabilities with a lot of potential value, but until these data capabilities are applied, the value in them is unrealized.

Data Value is the outcome we aim to maximize through Data Leadership, and is the most important consideration for data and technology efforts anywhere in our businesses. This is our North Star—if we can find it, we will find our way.

Think of Data Value as the ultimate measure of the true benefits our data sprockets and widgets give to our customers. This depends not just on what we provide to them, but how well they turn the potential value into real outcome.

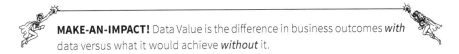

MAKE-AN-IMPACT! Data Value is the difference in business outcomes *with* data versus what it would achieve *without* it.

Realize that Data Value is not really about data at all. It is about the positive change in business outcomes we are able to make happen by using data. And just as important is understanding the inverse relationship: if our actions create no positive differential in business outcomes, then we have done nothing of value. In more practical terms, if we deliver a report that fails to change anybody's behavior (and thus creates no change in business outcome), then how could the real resources we used in creating that report be justified?

MAKE-AN-IMPACT! Data Leadership influences, but does not control, Data Value.

Data Value is the barometer by which we should judge our Data Leadership performance, and it extends to everyone and everything working with information in our businesses, regardless of whether or not they identify as Data Leaders. It is not enough to have information. It is not even enough to use the information to do something. The information must drive a result with consequences (hopefully positive ones!). Like anything we do with data, maximizing our outcomes begins with measuring.

MAKE-AN-IMPACT! Data Value is measured in three ways:

1. Increasing revenue

2. Decreasing cost

3. Managing risk

These are the *only* ways Data Value gets created.

Increasing revenue and decreasing costs should be relatively obvious—money in and money out. Managing risk is treated separately because risk management effectiveness cannot be measured by looking directly at results—the sample size of events that actually happen is too small to gauge the proper insurance strategy. Things become a little more sophisticated to get that piece right, but to start with, we can focus our energies on increasing revenue and decreasing costs.

Also note that dollars and other hard currencies may not be the only unit of measure, since the objectives of an organization may be to provide another outcome, such as a public service or charitable function. If we think of "increasing revenue" as the organization's ability to deliver more of that service or function, "decreasing costs" as improving the operating efficiency of delivery, and "managing risk" as managing risk—then we are all set! We may need to do a little semantic translation of some of the concepts, but Data Value very much applies in any type of organization.

Priorities will vary, as will the appropriate balance of what will be needed to maximize Data Value, but that's why we are "Data Leaders!" If creating Data Value were as simple in practice as in concept, we'd just be "Data Middle-of-the-Packers." Because we're setting a high bar, let's make sure we understand the Data Value concept completely.

First, consider a simple example:

Sales data for a restaurant is correlated with weather conditions using a simple regression model. Tomorrow's forecast is for unseasonably cool temperatures, so the owner decides that they will need one fewer lobster in the tank. A few dollars are saved, and Pinchy lives to fight another day. So in this simple (but heartfelt) example, costs are decreased directly due to data analysis.

Now for a more complicated scenario:

Company B has decided to sponsor a project that will, among other things, perform a data lineage analysis for a set of core executive reports. The executive team uses these reports already, but has identified inconsistencies in some of the numbers, and this has led to a general sense of distrust in the organization's data.

What will the value be of performing this data lineage analysis? Could be a lot of things, right? Perhaps once the executives regain their trust in the data, they will be able to make decisions more quickly, exploiting new business opportunities (increase revenue). Or once the differences in numbers are better understood, they will reduce the effort spent manually reconciling everything (decrease costs). The managing risks possibility is obvious as well.

Here's the thing: it's not enough to identify where the value might come from. It is imperative to take a baseline measurement of the current situation, and then measure again and compare once the project is complete. It may not be possible to get a fully quantitative measurement, but even a ballpark/order-of-magnitude assessment is better than relying on people's selective memory the next time we want to propose a Data Value-enhancing project.

In our report example, we could directly measure the amount of time being spent on report creation, plus how much time it takes to reconcile the non-matching numbers. We could survey the executives to determine their current level of trust in the data, and how willing they are to use data to drive their decisions and activities—and that will help us link to the data's measurable difference in business outcomes. Even if the measurements are subjective, we can at least quantify our impacts down the road once additional efforts are underway.

If we fail to benchmark, we lose an opportunity to measure Data Value. Worse, we lose the ability to make our own efforts as efficient and impactful as possible. By always pushing to understand the real Data Value, we will hopefully avoid the activities that feel like productive work but actually fail to produce results.

MAKE-AN-IMPACT! Never confuse potential value with real value. "Busy" is not the same as "productive."

Data Governance is a common endeavor for organizations that want to do more with data, which we will talk about at various points later in the book. As an example, if we set up a Data Governance organization, we are committing to a lot of effort with several degrees of separation between the Data Governance activities and the three ways value is actually created. This likely creates a lot of potential value, but the realized value of Data Governance is notoriously difficult to quantify.

Before we start to question why anybody tries to do Data Governance at all, do know that creating potential Data Value is still incredibly important. We devote a significant part of this book to all of the ways we create potential Data Value. But even if we have all the potential in the world, not unlike the next overhyped sports star—if we can't put points on the board, our potential will be quickly forgotten.

The difference between potential value and realized value is just like scoring points in sports. Sure, the way we keep score in the business world is a little different than sports, but to create real Data Value, our efforts must result in something that impacts organizational success. If data is not driving meaningful, measurable changes in business outcomes, then the data provides no value. It is really that simple. End of book. Thanks for reading.

Just kidding! We've got like 18 more chapters of saying this over and over again in different ways. Stay with me, because if we explore further we will get some fantastic ideas on how to measure and maximize our organization's ability to realize Data Value. It really isn't enough to just know what Data Value is. The tricky part is maximizing that value, and that starts with measuring it. At least this part is easy in concept!

The preceding examples illustrate how these three measurements of Data Value are often hiding in plain sight—they are usually there, but many times we do not either know to or choose to take the time to track them.

MAKE-AN-IMPACT! One of the great ironies of the Data Management space is that we often fail to measure our own performance the way we advocate everybody else does.

I think this may be due to the several degrees of separation that exists from Data Value-driven projects and increasing revenue, decreasing costs, and managing risks. We do things, and then somebody else does something, then one more person does something, and *then* Data Value is realized, maybe. And after all this we wonder why Data Governance projects struggle? Too often they do not even bother trying to justify their existence!

MAKE-AN-IMPACT! Data projects of any kind will not be successful unless we demonstrate overwhelmingly the value being added by our efforts.

It is unfortunate that there are so many steps between our data efforts and tangible business value, but that's how it is. This is also why Data Management is commonly misunderstood, and those of us dedicating our careers to it are having such incredible adventures transforming our organizations!

There are simpler paths to personal career success. There are more financially-lucrative ones. However, there are no roles more central to the success of organizations across all industries than that of the Data Leader. Our titles and specific responsibilities will vary, but our commitment to creating Data Value will prove to be one of the most influential differentiators of tomorrow's businesses.

The rest of this book will help you build the perspective and skills to create Data Value, and we will refer back to this chapter's concepts frequently. Consider this book your sharpening stone to realign your focus on what matters when the real world proves distracting. Here we will talk about how things *should* be, and what you *should* do in response. In practice, it is never so clear, and every decision comes with a tradeoff. We all have day jobs and responsibilities, never enough time or resources, office politics, people that don't get it, people that don't care, and if we're lucky, personal lives we like to have occasionally.

So let's take a breath, maybe softly whisper "Data Value" to ourselves a couple times, and then turn the page—both literally and figuratively. It is not trivial to be at the center of our organization's future success, and many of us may not have intended to be here. If nothing else, remember that here we are among friends, and that if we fail to deliver Data Value, our companies are doomed. No pressure!

2 WHAT WE SHOULD DO DIFFERENTLY

Data Value makes good sense. It is logical, measurable, and a concept that we can drive a whole bunch of meaningful activities from. Lucky for us, because many of our organizations are currently operating as if they have no clue why they are doing many of the data-related activities that consume so much time, energy, and financial resources.

This current lack of understanding of Data Value is evident through the interactions of our business and technology personnel. While technology has always had an order-taker role, the communications between these two groups is often inefficient at best, and commonly completely dysfunctional.

The process looks something like this:

- The business person will ask a technology person for something like a report or new data-centric application. Most technology initiatives with funding start with the business having an idea of something they want.

- There will be some back-and-forth ironing out all of the business "requirements" to ensure that there is enough detail to drive a technical specification.

- To gain better understanding of what the business person is looking for, the technology persons will at some point ask questions like: "How will you use this?," "What will you use this for?," "How will this help you?," "What do you need from this?," and "What are your business requirements?"

- The business responds with some amount of detail, and often there are a couple rounds of revisions. At some point the team feels that the design is complete, and then the technology people go into their caves, emerging some time later with a solution that checks all the boxes.

In an "agile" shop, the tech team may emerge more frequently with smaller improvements, but that doesn't really matter here. The fact is that they already botched the design, so however they want to build the wrong thing doesn't change the fact that they are building the wrong thing.

Based on our definition of Data Value, did you catch where in this typical process they lost their way?

It was when IT asked the business what they want. Asking those "What do you want?" type of questions comes from a one-sided perspective, and leads to an inability to gauge value, drive priorities, or have a meaningful two-way collaboration about the design of what is being built.

MAKE-AN-IMPACT! When we phrase our design questions looking only at the end point, we lose our ability to maximize the differential in business outcomes because we have no benchmark of the starting point.

Nothing better reflects this than "business requirements." As a term and as a philosophy, business requirements should be banished to the recycle bin of history. We could not choose a more one-directional, condescending, yet sadly accurate label to illustrate the current state of business/technology interactions. The concept of business requirements is completely opposed to everything we should stand for as Data Leaders. Please allow me to explain.

The way it typically works is business requirements are mapped in detail by a business analyst, which leads to a technical design that accommodates those requirements, and that leads to the people who build it all. Some of these tasks can be performed by the same people in roles that crossover, but there are usually multiple people involved as it progresses. Regardless of precisely how many people or steps are involved, outcomes suffer when the flow of information is too one-directional.

How many technology systems have been adversely impacted because the business never gave IT a voice in design? Countless. I can promise you with 95 percent likelihood that in your organization there is more than one technologist who has given up trying to do their best work because any time they suggest an alternative to a business requirement-driven design element, they are told to just get it done as originally specified.

As we defined earlier, Data Value comes from the difference in business outcomes. The only way to gauge that difference is to measure (or estimate) the starting and ending outcomes. Any project that relies only on vague directional guidance like "It will improve our customer service" or "The current system is too slow" is going to have suboptimal outcomes.

MAKE-AN-IMPACT! We should not ask, "What do you want?" or equivalent. We should instead ask, "How do we create a solution that maximizes the improvement in business outcomes compared with the costs of developing that solution?"

Granted, that may be a bit of a mouthful for one question, but the goal is to ask a series of questions to fully understand the following:

- What is the starting point? What would the situation be if we do nothing? What are the likely business outcomes in the continuing status quo situation?

- How does the business envision its outcomes improving with this effort? Are there specific business outcome goals in mind? Who is responsible for these outcomes? Is that individual sponsoring this project effort? How will we measure the results for both the resources consumed as well as impacts to revenues, costs, and risk management?

- How do the known costs align with available resources, given the current design? What is not yet known that the success of this project may depend upon?

Now we are directly addressing the value of data! We are having a conversation to predict the expected impact to revenue, cost, and risk mitigation. If we ask about a differential in outcome, we will establish a current baseline and a clear target result for the endeavor. Any specific design elements get calibrated against Data Value, and that leads us down a path to getting the benefits maximized compared to the costs of making it happen.

Perhaps more importantly, it begins to change the dynamics of the relationship between the business (requestor) and technology (requestee) from a one-directional flow to a two-way collaboration. When we talk about maximizing the ultimate outcomes to the business, we become a team—mutually committed to finding the right path to the greatest business impact.

This is a departure from how things work in many organizations. Technology (and data) folks like to focus on their functional responsibilities, and often do not get deep enough into the business impacts of what they do. On the flip side, when business people are in charge of providing requirements to build new systems, they often define what they want in terms of what they have, and this will limit their ability to create innovative solutions that make the most of the latest technology capabilities that the technology folks really, really want to put to use!

MAKE-AN-IMPACT! Technology folks have a tremendous knowledge of what is possible, which directly complements the business' in-depth understanding of what would be useful.

The partnership *should be* amazing! It is like peanut butter and jelly, or peanut butter and chocolate, or peanut butter and celery! (I sure like peanut butter, apparently.) But for some reason, the IT and business groups often have less-than-stellar working relationships—and if we want to maximize Data Value, that's something we are going to need to address.

3 BRIDGING THE DIVIDE BETWEEN IT AND THE BUSINESS

We are going to get this out of the way early, since this dynamic is central to many of the challenges we face in the data space. It boils down to this:

MAKE-AN-IMPACT! Data is the very essence of our businesses, held in complete control by information technology professionals.

Just reading that sentence makes us feel uneasy, doesn't it? We probably agree by now that data is pretty important, so if we want to be a bit dramatic and call it the "very essence of our businesses" we can probably get away with that. The second part is the scary part—we are not so comfortable turning over something so important to those IT people. The problem is, you know, that it was the information systems that captured the data in the first place. It was *always* in control of the IT systems! The rest of us just finally recognized how important data really is!

Now it isn't a huge stretch to suggest that "the business" and "IT" do not generally get along great. But why has it gotten so bad? Don't we realize how much we need each other? Do I need to talk about peanut butter some more?

I have an opinion. Note that the following is highly subjective, a bit sensationalized, but earnestly drawn from decades of experience observing this dynamic relationship from several roles.

My perspective on the perspective of the IT folks:

IT people, of which I identify myself as one, often see themselves as superheroes. We take insane requests from the business and use our technical wizardry to do magical things that nobody actually appreciates, but should rightfully strike everyone to their core with awe. We get judged in black-and-white, while everybody else around here never seems to have any clear performance metrics. Everybody wants everything done immediately, with no respect for our systems development lifecycle (SDLC)—but whenever the smallest thing goes wrong it's Information Technology's fault.

It's like we are being singled-out and treated differently than everybody else. Those business folks never appreciate the complexity and the fact that we always manage to get stuff done, even though we've never been given the budget to address the looming technical debt that keeps growing after years of inadequate support from the business!

And now my perspective on the perspective of the business-side:

Business people, which I also identify as (I'm functionally ambidextrous), are perpetually frustrated with IT folks. The IT people seem to only ever say "no," and even items that should be simple fixes take weeks or months, if they ever get addressed at all.

IT people are always complaining about being under-resourced, but the business does not have the resources to keep dumping into the vortex of technology when our ROI on these investments is questionable at best. Lots of times, when things do get done, they have a bunch of stability/reliability issues and what they deliver may not even resemble what we wanted in the first place!

The IT people are constantly doing "maintenance" and "patch fixes" that never seem to do anything other than cause outages. We have a business to run, and too often we are held hostage by IT!

And end scene.

Like I disclaimed, my scenarios may have been a bit sensationalized, but we could all likely relate to at least some of it. This mutual animosity between IT and the business has built up over decades of poor communication and a genuine lack of empathy among the different areas of our organizations. Because the pattern is so consistent, these feelings naturally transfer across different companies, so even getting new personnel will do little to remedy these chronic issues.

So we're going to start over. Even though I believe everything we've covered in this chapter so far is true, we need to forget it. We can't start here if we want to transform our organizations into nimble, high-functioning, data-driven organizations. We need to fix things even further upstream. So, let's address the question that everybody should have been asking from the start of this:

Is this really how we should break down our organizations?

MAKE-AN-IMPACT! It is ridiculous that we bisect our organizations into the "Information Technology (IT)" department and literally everybody else in the company. IT is part of the business, just like every other department in the business.

Kind of seems like we are singling out the technology folks and treating them differently than the rest of the folks. Maybe this is why IT people feel like they are being singled out and treated differently than the rest of the folks.

In defense of *the rest of the folks*, technology people tend to be a bit different, and do not always respond well when the business does try to communicate better. The tech people do voodoo with their JSON and APIs and Python and other strangely-titled things they go to conferences to learn about. For instance, "Splunk" can't be a real thing, can it?

Maybe if these people are kept locked in their windowless caves in the basement and we pay them pretty well, then they won't run off and leave the business folks to try to deal with it all. They will keep doing their jobs and keep the lights on and the systems running, and the business will get a new report or self-service data visualization tool once in a while.

This is not at all irrational. People are busy and focused on their own jobs, and not on how to gain the most competitive advantage by leveraging the nerds who don't like to talk to people. This used to be okay, back when individual servers were the size of rooms, and you didn't have a supercomputer in your pocket at all times. The demands of today's businesses require much more than you can do on your own, and those IT folks hold the keys to your future success.

Remember Data Value? Try creating some of that without relying on IT in some way. Also, please note, while I recognize it is against my principles to continue to refer to these groups as "IT" and "the business," there is a lot of work to be done before we can say those divisions no longer exist. So to make things simpler throughout this book, I'll continue using it. Just know I don't like it, and hopefully in the next edition I will be able to say "the business" and "the business" and then it will all be super-clear to everybody. Until then, begrudgingly, I'm going to keep talking about "IT" and "the business."

An organization has a few choices when considering how to address the conflict between IT and the business:

- **Ignore it and Hope for the Best:** This is the current approach employed by many businesses. It isn't working so far, but maybe things will turn around once the technology improves. That's a silly thought, but it's not silly to consider doing nothing. In fact, this is something we must always consider whenever we are attempting to create Data Value—and repairing the relationship between IT and the business is certainly part of that!

  The benefits of this approach are that we can use our efforts in a more targeted way elsewhere, and that we aren't asking everybody to change how they work. The downside is that we do not fix the underlying problem and that this dysfunction will act like a tax, hurting every other initiative involving both IT and the business. Rats! This plan was sounding so good two sentences ago.

- **Redefine the Relationship:** The term "cross-functional teams" comes to mind. If we want IT and the business to start acting like one business, maybe it makes sense to mash them together and make them do everything as a team. This way they'll hopefully start to de-velop empathy for one another and teach each other some new skills while they are at it.

  The strength of this approach is that it directly addresses the root cause of the divide between IT and the business—that they have little empathy for one another because they do not really understand what the other does. If done well, this will transform your organization by supercharging productivity, employee satisfaction and retention, and likely get us promoted. The downside of this approach is that it is supremely disruptive to people's status quo, and if not proactively managed, we will encounter decreased productivity, lower employee satisfaction, higher attrition, and a fair chance that it fails entirely and we end up no better or worse than before. We'll also probably get fired.

- **Blow it Up Completely:** Some organizations see that they shouldn't choose Door Number 1, and Door Number 2 seems too risky, so they have tried to find a better path. An industry has developed that allows our organizations to outsource any of our IT-related functions, and because the folks performing the services are external to our own companies, they presumably will try harder to perform well and keep the rest of us happy.

  Positives include that this approach typically comes with some cost-savings, either due to an offshoring arrangement, or simply the economies-of-scale that the vendor firm has by spreading their systems, personnel, and practices across multiple clients. Outsourcing IT responsibilities may give our companies the ability to flex more effectively, aligning the size of project teams to fit the increased demand of building something, and then ramping down when in more of a maintenance mode. Also, attracting the talent we'd like to have internally may simply not be feasible. Public-sector organizations, for example, often have difficulty recruiting the full-time talent they need, so the next-best option is to bring in contractor assistance to help get the job done.

  The negative with this approach is that an outsourcing strategy can create operational or strategic disconnects between the business itself and the systems and data the business relies upon to be a business. Think of it this way: if data represents the essence of an organization, and we outsource the technical responsibilities related to it, are we in danger of effectively selling our souls?

So what should we do? Well, it depends. The answer is going to look a little different for every organization, but most will probably have parts of each of the above strategies. Frankly, the specific approach above matters far less than the intent of those involved.

If you can align people's interests in such a way that they are committed to working together to make your company awesome, then use whatever interaction coordination mechanism you like.

Now that we understand the basics of the problem and the three main ways to address it, we find ourselves in need of some good, old-fashioned leadership. This can sometimes be accomplished purely by leaders outside the technology organization, but typically it is best to involve IT leadership in this kind of transformation. It may not be the *same* IT leadership that got us into the mess in the first place—but if we choose a path that involves people needing to change, we are going to need help wherever we can find it.

It's easy (and kinda fun) to blame all of these challenges of IT solely on our technology personnel—after all, they need to be responsible for their own jobs. The CIOs sit at the top of the technology pyramid, so they rightfully get the lion's share of the blame. We will not correct the broken dynamics between IT and the rest of the business unless our CIOs do a better job of contributing business-relevance at the senior-most levels of our organizations. That is obviously necessary, and should be the first thing we change.

Don't hold your breath.

Asking a CIO to all-of-a-sudden be a capable business leader is like asking a fish to go for a jog around the lake. CIOs have spent 20 to 30 years working in technology—they are typically ill-equipped to do the jobs we are asking of them. Spending a career in this mess is not the way to change things—and remember, these breakdowns between IT and the business are not entirely IT's fault, so it's just not reasonable to expect our CIOs to magically have it all figured out despite being in the middle of it all for their entire careers.

When I teach basic management training, the first tenet I explain to students is that for each one of your employees, you must balance the empowerment you give them with the accountability you are asking of them. In other words, you must put people in a position to be successful—the more you need from them, the more control you must cede to them.

MAKE-AN-IMPACT! We cannot ethically hold someone accountable for something we never gave them the opportunity to do.

If you want to see the most egregious examples of this, go find a CISO (Chief Information Security Officer). Few have the ability to implement the controls they desire, but all are first under the bus the moment a breach happens. I think some organizations have that position simply to have a convenient person to blame when things go sideways.

Take the CISO, move a step higher up the food chain, and you have the situation many CIOs find themselves in. They sit at the top of often-large departments, where their primary responsibility is often to be the top technology order-taker and scapegoat.

For those of us who haven't had this kind of role in an organization, this may seem extreme. Let's consider this: who does the CFO call if her laptop is slow, or who does an Executive Vice-President call when her Outlook keeps crashing on startup? Some will properly delegate to their assistants or call the helpdesk themselves—but when it's really important to them that things get fixed fast, the CIO gets that call directly, every time.

As much as we'd like to change things starting with the CIO, it's going to take more than that. Today's challenges are the result of decades of poor engagement between the business and IT, and to change it we are going to have to teach our CIOs to become business leaders. This will only happen if they are given an opportunity to learn and partner with the business (empowerment) as they deliver the Data Value necessary to empower business outcomes (accountability).

So it's clear that things aren't working between IT and everybody else. If we realign to embracing our shared responsibility of maximizing Data Value—and focus on how we can maximize business outcomes together, then we'll start to improve this dysfunctional relationship. Preaching Data Value won't be enough. After all, how many business or technology people are really committed to shifting a long-held paradigm of systemic ineffectiveness in communication between diverse sets of stakeholders?

I'm not sure most people would be committed enough to carefully read that last sentence, let alone do something about it. So we should probably just give up and deal with the fact that business and IT folks are incompatible and we're all doomed.

Of course not! We're going to fix this! But we've got to break it down before we build it back up, so now seems as good a time as any to hit rock bottom. It is about one crucially important fact that we all must keep in mind if we want people to do something:

MAKE-AN-IMPACT! The number one lesson of human motivation is that nobody cares about you.

What you need, your great ideas, your kids, your important projects, your future, your vacation, your blah-blah-blah. When we talk, most of the time people are filtering every single one of our words through their "how does this impact me" lens. They will smile and nod all day until something we are saying hits close enough to home. Realize that people, out of some evolutionary necessity, really only care about adding benefits, lessening pain, or managing risk on their own personal level.

Unless we are talking about truly charitable acts done for the benefit of humanity by people who have a strong personal motivation to make these contributions—*and it's a trap!* Seemingly charitable acts are still personally motivated by people who want to feel good about themselves and their contributions—these are just not *monetarily* motivated self-interests. Did we just inadvertently disparage charitable acts? Not at all, but we did acknowledge that even helping others traces its underlying motivations to serving ourselves.

It's okay, though, don't give up yet! Self-interested motivations gives us something to work with because we can reasonably expect that if we can appeal to selfish individuals (i.e., all of us), then we can effect change. If we are capable of achieving positive net impacts, regardless of the motivations, then we will be able to achieve Data Value creation. And isn't that the most important thing?

Yes. That time it wasn't a trick—good job!

 MAKE-AN-IMPACT! When incentives are aligned to the motivations of those whose behavior we want to influence, and if asks are aligned with the empowerment, and the net benefits outweigh the net pain, then people will accomplish amazing things.

Data Leadership is fundamentally rooted in this truth, and we will spend a lot of time in the remaining chapters discussing techniques to achieve it. We must always remember that people are watching out for #1 more than anything else, and if we are going ask them to do something, there had better be something in it for them, too! This could be as little as pizza, or as much as a partnership. Or a jet.

I've never actually seen the jet one, but I'm sure it has happened for somebody. Now that's a good motivational goal! Increase sales by 50 percent and you get a jet! People would run through brick walls like the Kool-Aid Man to avoid flying commercial. Oh yeah!

Sadly, however, "benefitting the organization's profitability" rarely provides enough motivation to get people to do more than attend a meeting or two. We will have to be more creative if we want data-driven initiatives to take flight. We'll get into this more later, but even expecting people to act in their own best interests is an oversimplification. People will more easily act from fun or convenience, and yes, even will on occasion act out of wanting to help somebody. Selfishly wanting to help somebody, usually, but hey, we'll take what we can get!

Earlier we talked about balancing empowerment with accountability within our teams. The same holds true as we work with areas outside our direct organizational lines. If you happen to be, or aspire to be a Chief Data Officer, you will find that as your profile raises, so does the percentage of time you spend trying to manage or influence initiatives that span far beyond your direct teams.

One of the most prevalent and failure-ridden of these endeavors is that of Data Governance. Most organizations attempting Data Governance today are on their third or fourth ride on this merry-go-round. Sadly, most still have no chance of succeeding. In the upcoming chapter, we talk about how to rethink this whole Data Governance thing that so many of us get worked up about.

4 THE TRUTH ABOUT DATA GOVERNANCE

We have been talking about the breakdowns between the business and technology folks in an organization, and we identified the challenges around incentives and motivating people. These all become big factors as we try to keep Data Governance's momentum going, but they are not why most Data Governance is flawed out of the gate.

Since some of us may not know much about Data Governance beyond the couple references in this book, let's start with a definition. This is probably a good idea for everybody here, in fact, because it seems like this Data Management space has a wide variety of definitions. Here's mine:

MAKE-AN-IMPACT! Data Governance is how we coordinate people to help our organizations get the most from our data.

This typically leads us to clarify definitions, provide data lineage maps, and generally try to make things more transparent so people spend less time asking and answering questions about the data—and spend more time asking and answering questions with the data.

I think the definition above is what we should be aiming for with Data Governance—yet when we observe Data Governance in the wild, it seems that many organizations' working definition of Data Governance is: "Have sparsely-attended meetings to create data rules that nobody else knows or cares about, and to complain that people do not understand or appreciate what we are trying to do with Data Governance."

And based on the above definition, did we just do some Data Governance ourselves by clarifying definitions? You betcha. We didn't even need twelve people in a meeting to talk about it! That crack on pointless meetings may feel a little harsh, but in reality the most common pattern of Data Governance attempts in organizations looks something like this:

- Executive sponsor gets excited about data, decides to do Data Governance (again) but get it right this time.

- Go-getters (aspiring Data Leaders) do a bunch of hard work to get things moving.

- The Data Governance program is launched with great fanfare.

- Data Governance council meets, often monthly, starting with near-universal participation with the exception of an executive or two who don't really understand why they are there.

- At each meeting data is talked about, next steps are defined, and people are assigned tasks.

- Between meetings, sometimes people get done what they were assigned, but often they "didn't have time"—but *this month* they will absolutely get to it.

- Over time, meeting attendance diminishes and/or the meeting frequency slows down because there is not enough for the council to do.

- After 12 to 24 months, the whole thing sort of fades away, and nobody seems to notice.

Many Data Governance programs end up as pointless, half-complete, miserable uses of people's time and energy, while they last. If we identify the purpose of most Data Governance endeavors, it comes down to some mashup like "making data a more transparent, usable asset that helps facilitate business operations and ensure compliance with regulatory mandates."

Is that a helpful undertaking? Of course.

Will it ever work? Nope. Why in the world would we focus Data Governance this way?

Sadly, this general pattern happens more than it doesn't. What's the problem here? Why doesn't this top-down Data Governance model seem to work?

MAKE-AN-IMPACT! Getting a bunch of folks together in a room to talk about data creates no Data Value by itself.

Putting together policies, establishing data owners, documenting data definitions—none of these directly create Data Value. And frankly, these are so many steps removed from actual Data Value creation that most Data Governance organizations have no idea how much net positive impact their efforts have on the business. C'mon! We need to be better than that.

Will it be important to have some meetings to talk about data? Probably. But we need more direction and more concrete outcomes. We need accountability to balance the empowerment, and we'd better find a way to impact the business, quickly.

MAKE-AN-IMPACT! We don't need Data Governance, we *need* to create Data Value. Data Governance is part of how we do that.

Data Governance should remove friction from everything we do with data. If we can quickly and clearly reference the definition of a data element, that can save us a lot of time and energy, helping us continue on our path unabated. But what if we aren't yet moving? A frictionless environment doesn't do us a lot of good.

In fact, Data Governance in the absence of other momentum is like an '83 Ford Mustang convertible with bald tires in the middle of an icy parking lot in February—it's not helping us get anywhere. But in a few months when the weather is nice we will be so glad we have it because it will be so useful then—and that's exactly when the motor gives out completely and we have to go back to riding our bicycles!

MAKE-AN-IMPACT! Doing Data Governance to address some future pain or to help solve some ambiguous future efficiency goal is simply a subtle way to avoid accountability—instead, find a way to add Data Value now.

Chances are to do this, Data Governance will be involved in some way, so let's build it over time in alignment with the actual value it contributes. But what if we don't have the option to take a ninja-like approach to building Data Governance? What if we have been told that Data Governance is what we need to do as our job? What if we are doing lots of things with data, have plenty of momentum, and Data Governance is really what we need to remove friction so that we can work better with data?

That's great! We certainly want to do Data Governance if it is well-justified, but it is important for people to realize that we should be deliberate in our objectives with Data Governance. It is not an end unto itself, but must be used judiciously as means-to-an-end. In fact, within the Data Leadership Framework that we cover soon, Data Governance is not even designated as a separate discipline. This is because Data Governance is everywhere data is, involved with everything we do with data, both organizationally and individually.

Bob Seiner starts many of his talks by asking the audience who in the room has Data Governance in their organization. Around half the room will raise their hands. Then Bob tells everyone to raise their hands because every organization is governing data somehow. It just may not be well-organized, coordinated, or effective. His point is that some set of norms and expectations, even if not proactively managed, still influences folks' data-related behaviors—and we will accomplish far more with our data if we put some structures in place so those norms and expectations are more consistent and reliable.

I agree with Bob, as well as the other Data Governance experts out there, and I believe that Data Leadership is actually a complement to their works—the other side of the same coin, if you will. While Data Governance provides guidance, it does not inherently build momentum, which is *exactly* what Data Leadership is designed to do.

MAKE-AN-IMPACT! Data Governance always exists, but it does not accomplish very much without Data Leadership.

The converse of the above is that Data Leadership doesn't accomplish *anything* without Data Governance (which fortunately for us, always exists in some form). And we definitely will get more done with Data Leadership if we have competent Data Governance. So though it is not a part of Data Leadership, Data Governance is crucial to Data Leadership's success.

Knowing this, we should have a baseline understanding of how to do Data Governance in support of Data Leadership. We should also understand that it is likely that our organizations are starting with some amount of formalized Data Governance, whereas it is far less likely that they already have a focused Data Leadership program in place.

So it is reasonable that we spend a little time going through Data Governance fundamentals— and even for the seasoned pros out there, this section may have a slightly different perspective from the norm. To get Data Governance right, we must start at the beginning by asking what is triggering the call for Data Governance in an organization. First, let's think about banks.

Banks are great. You give them your money, and then they give it back when you need it. Some even pay you a few cents a month for the privilege, while others make you pay them to loan them your money. Doesn't that sound like a great business model? Having people pay fees to lend them money. How does any bank ever go out of business?

The banking industry has attracted some unwanted attention related to fraud and mortgage-backed securities, among other crises over the years, and these have resulted in a healthy amount of regulation. Legislation like Dodd-Frank and Sarbanes-Oxley in the U.S. have added a fair amount of complexity to how banks must operate—and importantly, outlines some of the controls that must exist to protect the stability of the banking system. One of these controls is that banks must have Data Governance. Though the preceding sentence is not directly quoting the regulation, the lack of precision is about the same.

Regulators are typically not deep Data Governance experts, but someone suggested it, and the provision sounded good to them at the time. I actually met one of these regulators at a conference once, and I asked him how they create these regulations. He glanced around the room, leaned toward me slightly, and softly said that they write something intentionally vague but with some directional guidance, and then wait to see how the companies react—and when the regulators see something they like, they point to it and tell others to do it that way too!

This blew my mind, but after thinking about it for a while it makes perfect sense—and thus regulatory mandates like this are one way Data Governance gets off the ground. When a governing body tells us that we must comply with confusing mandates or there will be fines or other penalties, then our executives will usually sanction efforts to comply.

MAKE-AN-IMPACT! Regulatory origins for Data Governance are a common—but dangerous—way to spearhead Data Governance efforts.

Regulatory-inspired Data Governance initiatives tend to focus on compliance above all else, and never amount to more than a necessary cost of doing business. These will tend to focus on checking the right boxes, assigning people to roles and definitions to terms, and is largely an exercise in satisfying regulators who don't even understand it all in the first place. People involved feel obligated to do things, but their hearts are not in it—and the entire program is considered a necessary evil. Data Governance can be so much more!

MAKE-AN-IMPACT! Data Governance should not exist simply to go through the motions—Data Governance must help the organization operate better through the effective use of data.

This is the other origin story for Data Governance: when it is created to drive Data Value, and therefore created to promote Data Leadership. Coupling Data Governance to Data Leadership still satisfies the regulatory hurdles, but also creates momentum. This leads to an easier program to keep running, as it is not simply a cost of doing business or necessary evil.

With Data Leadership-inspired Data Governance, executives can get excited about a positive return-on-investment, and this enables us to align incentives in a motivating way for all those involved. Even in regulated environments, creating Data Governance capabilities with an innovation mindset is the best way to maximize Data Value.

So now we understand what should be awfully-similar motivations between starting Data Governance and promoting Data Leadership. One early step to making either a reality is to get some support from the top. Executive sponsorship is a crucial component to creating something with enough scale to have a real impact. As we'll learn later, we do not need executive backing to demonstrate the potential of what we will do, but we sure will need their help to make it a full reality.

It's important to realize that executives typically live in circumstances where positive gains are nice and helpful, and *potentially* rewarding, but unexpected negative outcomes will be severely punished. Executives obviously want to support good ideas, but they also have a well-honed self-preservation instinct to distance themselves from failure. They also like to be associated with growth and new initiatives that have had no time to lose their luster—so while it is a necessary and laudable achievement to get top people to the

Data Governance kickoff, what is truly impressive is when they have been continually involved a year later.

Despite what people on a lower rung may want to believe, executives are not stupid. We should give them a little credit: at least they were willing to stick their necks out far enough to recognize and support our data initiatives in the first place! But once things get going, most will delegate to us to keep things moving along while they turn their direct attention to other things. They simply do not have enough time in the day to be hands-on with every function that rolls up to them.

What we haven't yet covered is the make-up of the Data Governance council, or equivalent group in our organization. If we stack the Data Governance council with a bunch of high-ranking executives, we will have all the organizational firepower we need! The downside is that most senior folks are so busy they will rarely attend the meetings, and they are so far removed from the day-to-day interactions with data that they struggle with the detail demanded to perform effective Data Governance.

On the other hand, if we staff up our Data Governance council with a bunch of low-ranking folks that work with actual data all day, they will not have the organizational juice to make and enforce the necessary decisions made by Data Governance. So what should we do?

 MAKE-AN-IMPACT! The most successful Data Governance organizations tend to create a council with representation made up of senior and lower ranks in the organization.

The senior folks provide leadership and decision-making authority, and the lower-level folks have the detailed understanding to execute the tactical objectives effectively. Plus, it's pretty exciting for a Data Analyst to serve on a committee with the VP of Marketing—which means they will be highly-motivated not to mess up. Even if the senior folks don't make all the meetings personally, as long as they remain engaged, the Data Governance organization can be successful.

Now remember, just like everything in this book, we can establish guidelines—but the moment we go to apply them to an actual situation, things get complicated. It is imperative to work with what we have in our actual circumstances. All of the general rules outlined here have tradeoffs that may work in most situations, but not the one in which we actually find ourselves—tread carefully!

That said, there are some truths that arguably apply in every circumstance. Like if we do not have executive support and sponsorship for Data Governance, we as Data Leaders need to cultivate it. Nothing is scarier than executives running companies without any appreciation or reliance on the value of data. If our business leaders take an ostrich-like head-in-the-sand approach and want to ignore everything about data, then it might be a situation we can't fix, and we may want to find an organization that better shares our values.

If the executives appreciate that data has value, but are not sure what to do about it, we should first buy them a copy of this book (or five, just to be safe!), and then start working together to create Data Value! Data Governance activities will certainly be part of the answer, and not necessarily a bad way for us to get some involvement from our business leadership.

So, assuming that we have compiled the leadership of our Data Governance organization, and are ready to start doing something, watch out for the second trap that causes Data Governance to fail from the start: a focus on meetings.

When did meetings ever succeed as the place to get actual work done? Never! We cannot expect that Data Governance council meetings will magically become the first time we herded the cats into a windowless room, sometimes with snacks, and expect the outcome to be a tremendous Data Value creation.

MAKE-AN-IMPACT! Getting a group of middle-to-senior executives together to talk about data on a regular basis is not the recipe for spectacular data success.

Please understand, Data Governance council meetings serve an important purpose in coordinating and clarification, but that purpose does not have enough critical mass from the first day in your Data Governance efforts. To start with meetings creates a top-heavy Data Governance effort that will eventually buckle under its own weight.

The solution is to begin the real work in the trenches. Start with a training program to give necessary skills to those on whom our data efforts will rely. Get these people moving and collecting Metadata on the items we will need to make decisions, and then start mobilizing our decision-making competency on the Data Governance council.

Once the Data Governance council is formed and begins to meet, we only have one or two meetings to solidify their roles before people start losing interest and floating away. We must make sure that they have important, worthwhile things to do that give them a personal incentive to remain involved.

As the Data Governance organization starts to chalk up some wins, they will begin to drive their activities more independently. This momentum will allow us to take on more ambitious initiatives that will have ever-greater impacts on our organizations. We'll also be able to recruit more folks at all levels of the organization to jump on the bandwagon that is Data Governance.

As-if "Data Governance" weren't a sexy enough name for what we do, we also have the role of "data custodian," or its marginally-less-awfully-titled peer, the "data steward." For our purposes, these can be used interchangeably—though I'm sure somewhere the person that came up with these names is going to be enraged, just like the folks that get upset when I play loosey-goosey by interchanging terms like "information management" and "Data Management."

For the rest of us, these roles may not seem so glamorous. Cleaning up data and ensuring it can be used elsewhere in an organization is an arduous, often thankless job. Most people are not clamoring to sign up for these responsibilities, and for good reason—and a big reason Data Governance is often doomed from the start:

MAKE-AN-IMPACT! If we start Data Governance by asking people to help us, we are implying that our needs are more important than theirs.

People want to help one another, especially within our organizations, but when they see little personal gain from it they will not remain motivated to continue. Data Governance is often structured like a charity—please help us define and improve the quality of data so some future person's life will be a bit easier!

People mean well, but unless they are going to personally benefit, it will be tough to get continuing support for the long-term. Those being asked to help will quickly find the path of least resistance—which is to do just enough to not get yelled at. They will mostly stay under the radar, but this will weaken the foundation of our Data Governance efforts and ultimately erode participation until Data Governance just fades away completely. Sound familiar?

Experience shows us that, even under the best of circumstances, building lasting Data Governance is tough—but this imbalanced approach to Data Governance further hurts our chances for success. We must create an environment where our chances are maximized.

I prefer a bridge-builder analogy for a lot of what we do with data. Data people help connect different areas and needs of a business by building data and technology "bridges" between them. Data people don't necessary understand all of the ins-and-outs of the business traffic traversing the bridge, but we sure know how to build the bridges. Bad Data Governance often tries to build every bridge that can possibly be built, just in case somebody wants to drive over it someday.

If we were talking about real bridges, nobody would ever even attempt that (not even California!). Of course a build-every-conceivable-bridge program is going to fail spectacularly! So if the usual approach won't work, what should we do instead?

We should focus on Data Value. You knew I was going to say that, didn't you?

Who cares about Data Governance? It is simply a means to an end. That end is Data Value, as we defined at the start of this book.

MAKE-AN-IMPACT! We don't need Data Governance programs. We need Data Leadership programs that drive Data Value. We need to teach our businesses to use the data better to improve what they do.

Will we sneak some Data Governance in there? Absolutely. Doing Data Governance productively is more important than ever—but it must be done in the context of something that actually matters to people who would never willingly sign up for something called Data Governance. Though you probably should still give them a copy or five (just to be safe) of this book.

When we focus on Data Value first, we can identify how any individual might stand to gain by performing a data stewardship role. We can then motivate them to stay involved using the best motivator around: their own self-interest!

This cannot be overstated. One of the most common patterns of failing Data Governance efforts is focusing on persuading others to help *us* achieve *our* goals. We need to flip that around: Data Governance must exist to help *others* achieve *their* goals.

 MAKE-AN-IMPACT! When Data Governance takes a servant-leadership approach, it will find ways to connect to the business that it would have never found otherwise.

Remember the value of data—it is all rooted in the ability to measurably improve business outcomes. The more you serve to help a business achieve its objectives faster, or help calibrate already-in-progress initiatives, the more momentum you can build to take on the transformative opportunities that Data Analytics will uncover.

Earlier in this chapter we talked about how every organization currently has Data Governance, whether or not they actively manage it. What we must also recognize is that even the most competent Data Governance organizations will have some aspects of data that they are not actively managing. Not only is this okay, it is necessary. We won't be able to control it all—and if we try, we're simply going to create a terrible bottleneck that stifles productivity and innovation.

 MAKE-AN-IMPACT! We need to weave Data Leadership into an existing business to create data-driven change without being so disruptive that it hurts more than it helps.

Organizations need to crawl with data before they fly. Some businesses out there do not have much of an existing relationship with data today, so you'll need to start slowly. There is a time and place for massive, rapid changes, but those tend to come with collateral damage. People have a limit to how much change they are able to handle at one time. We must pick our spots, focus on Data Value, and get working on things that actually matter.

5 STOP TALKING ABOUT WORKING AND START WORKING

Anyone fortunate enough to have children, or spend much time around them, will be familiar with an occasional accident. This will either destroy something daddy or mommy loves, or cause some easily-avoidable injury to their siblings, or to the child themselves. Upon questioning, the perpetrator will inevitably respond, "But I didn't *mean* to!"

This never works. What kids and CEOs sometimes seem not to understand is that actions have consequences. Our intentions only matter when selecting and performing actions, but are no longer relevant when consequences have already occurred. We will be judged on outcomes alone—that, and how much people like working with us.

Perhaps you are interested in having a little more defensibility to your approach that may not work out quite as well as you hope. Or you are looking for more quantifiable evidence that your performance is as spectacular as you believe. Data will help in either of these use cases, and many, many more.

Data provides transparency between cause and effect—it brings us closer to the truth. This is why it is so upsetting when people choose to ignore it. Those folks will not be reading this, and they are going to find it harder and harder to remain relevant in a quickening world. So if you are on board with the relevance and potential of Data Analytics, what do you do first?

Answer: Anything other than have a meeting.

MAKE-AN-IMPACT! Great ideas never implemented will accomplish nothing compared to good ideas implemented well.

Momentum is built through motion and mass. Data Governance standards and policies have plenty of substance, but the motion part comes from taking action. As we mentioned in the last chapter, Data Leadership is how we'll build that motion, and in the next chapter we will introduce the Data Leadership Framework and begin to peel back the complexity of everything organizations can do to get the most from data.

We know we want to take action to make real differences, and we will cover the many disciplines necessary to accomplish all we want to achieve. These are not enough, however, to ensure lasting data success.

Actively building and managing momentum is paramount if we hope to keep data efforts alive. We cannot expect an if-you-build-it-they-will-come approach to succeed for any amount of time. People are fickle, and will not blindly serve the common good for long if those energies fail to give them something back. By actively solving for this challenge, we can give our efforts the chance of long-term success.

But there is a gap between completely organic, unmanaged Data Governance and the more robust Data Leadership Framework that has a lot going on.

MAKE-AN-IMPACT! What we need is something that helps get us started and moving along well enough to kick things into higher gear.

Fortunately, we have such a something. The Simple Virtuous Cycle reduces the complex topic of creating Data Value into its smallest, most atomic form. This cycle can be found inside most business processes, with multiple instances of varying scales working in harmony. As the world around us gets ever-more complex with new technologies and greater demands for data, we can distill them into this foundational cycle:

Simple Virtuous Cycle

The Simple Virtuous Cycle:

1. Measure

2. Identify Improvements

3. Improve

Everything we want to do in the world of data breaks out along these dimensions. The patterns are sadly common across all areas, as well:

4. **Measure:** Baseline and understand the complexities of the situation around us. Most of the time today this gets skipped completely.

5. **Identify Improvements:** Compile and quantify potential actions, and their range of likely outcomes. Most of the time today people advocate for what they intuitively feel is best and just run with it.

6. **Improve:** Implement the optimal actions as determined by the prior steps. Since measurements are a crucial part of the Simple Virtuous Cycle, any improvements should both drive Data Value and accommodate future measurements and improvement cycles. Most of the time today people are so focused on hard deliverables that they fail to prepare for future cycle iterations.

The Simple Virtuous Cycle can operate at large and small scales, but when starting out it is advantageous to try to make the cycles as small as possible. Think simple measurements, limited potential improvement options, easy improvements. Remember, this is about building momentum as much as it is about optimizing outcomes.

Why does this work? It keeps us focused on delivering Data Value at a fast pace. We must keep completing the cycle of value delivery to propel our organization forward. Think of this cycle as the wheels of a car spinning. Large efforts are akin to large wheels, taking longer to complete each revolution. At speed, large wheels may operate more efficiently by covering more ground with each revolution—but they are more costly to build and take more effort to get spinning in the first place.

Since a car can't practically change its wheel sizes, transmissions exist to change the gearing so that the engine's power can accelerate a car going different speeds. The more gears a transmission has, the more it can finely tune power delivery. A Continuously Variable Transmission (CVT) effectively does so without limit. The output of a CVT is like infinite variations of wheel sizes on a fixed axle.

This is why we start with small iterations that can get going with limited effort and resources. In Data Leadership we can always increase the size of the efforts over time as things get moving, just like a CVT in an automobile does. The Simple Virtuous Cycle similarly creates a self-reinforcing system that gets stronger (and bigger) as time goes on. When we have enough momentum, the full-fledged Data Leadership Framework will help us get wherever we want to go.

The other reason to start with this is that we do not need any specific domain expertise to get going. Yes, an advanced knowledge of Data Quality theory will help us implement a robust Data Quality scoring and remediation program at some point, but today we might know that the sales quantities that Finance is using are not reconciling to the totals from Operations. Why not dive into that one right now? Quantifying the high-level ROI should take about five seconds, and we will learn something new along the way, too!

After all, we won't change anything by talking about it. It is only by putting ourselves in motion that we can hope to transform our organizations. This also means that to be successful we will need to get people to change their behaviors.

To make things a little more complicated, simply changing peoples' behaviors will also not be enough. Effort is not the same thing as results. This seems obvious, but do not dismiss it—perhaps more than any other cause, time is wasted by "busy" people who foolishly believe that what they are doing matters. Despite having the best intentions, even the most talented among us can create negative value.

This is exemplified in how I came to have one of my most cherished office treasures: an autographed 2005 World Series baseball.

Every organization seems to have little things about their culture that makes the place unique. At one of my former employers, this took the form of people having balls that they would toss around or bounce against the walls. This could be mildly distracting, but mostly it was a little bit of simple stress-relief in a pretty intense place.

The balls that people owned seemed to be reflections of their personalities or what they cared about. Some had special meaning, and others were nothing more than the left-behinds of the person who used to have the office. One person had a racquetball that he would bounce against the wall to relieve stress, and another had a football that they'd flip up in the air to themselves or toss to another while solving the world's problems.

I saw this pattern, and because I wanted to fit in, I decided that I too should bring in a ball. Since I'm a White Sox fan, and I like to overthink even the simplest of decisions, I thought it might be fun to have a ball from the 2005 World Series, in which my beloved White Sox had their moment of glory by winning it all for the only time in my lifetime.

Seeing as how it was now over a decade later, I figured that would be the right mix of novelty and personal meaning to send the right message (beyond the one that I'm a data geek with a tendency to over-analyze everything).

At that time I did not actually own a 2005 World Series baseball, so I took to the internet to see what options I might have. A cursory evaluation on Amazon and eBay showed me what I would likely need to spend. If I wanted a plain, non-game-used baseball with the 2005 logo, it was running about $50. Game-used or autographed balls went up from there. A real treasure like a Paul Konerko-signed ball was in the $350 range, and a ball signed by the entire team got obscene—into four figures.

My "brilliant" idea appeared to be unrealistic—I mean, there was no way I was spending even $50 for this silly exercise. But I did think it would be fun to own a 2005 World Series ball, so I went back to the internet one last time to see if I could find something, anything, that would be less expensive.

That's when I stumbled upon it: an authentic 2005 World Series ball for only $20. And autographed, no less!

I thought it was a typo in the listing at first, but upon closer scrutiny I realized what was going on. This ball was listed by a sports memorabilia store that traded mostly in autographed items and other interesting sports stuff that collectors pay lots of money to acquire. Everything was supply/demand-based and the prices varied wildly based on how much people were willing to pay.

This is why the autographed ball was worth $20 in the market: it was signed by a Houston Astros rookie named Chris Burke. He ended up in the Major Leagues only for a handful of years, and his career ended in 2009. Not only did Houston lose the World Series in question, but it was signed by a person who most casual baseball fans would not recognize a decade later.

The Chris Burke-autographed 2005 World Series baseball may have been the best $20 I've ever spent. Not only did I get the ball I knew I wanted, marred slightly by a little bit of indecipherable blue ink, but I also received a bit of wisdom that continues to guide me today:

MAKE-AN-IMPACT! Adding energy to something is not the same as adding value.

When Chris Burke signed that ball in 2005, he certainly did not intend to decrease its market value by 60 percent. He reasonably thought that by scribbling on that ball, he'd be giving somebody a fine memento of a special event. Oh boy, did he ever!

Even today, that ball sits on my desk, and I often glance over at it or pick it up and toss it around while on calls or otherwise pondering some data-related challenge. It reminds me to carefully consider how my actions will result in real value, and not cause unintended negative outcomes.

Too few of our efforts are calibrated cautiously enough. It's not uncommon to see pointless meetings held, business glossaries go unused, standards and policies be ignored, or entire efforts stall due to ineffectiveness. How many organizations have rolled out entire new platforms without proper training for staff, and then are dismayed when it doesn't get the usage it deserves?

We are all surrounded by folks that equate being busy with being productive, and that is simply foolish. We each must force ourselves to think about the ball we are signing in our own work, and how all of our efforts in the data world are dependent on one another.

After all, the reason my autographed ball was worth so much less had nothing to do with how Chris Burke signs a baseball. By all measures, he has a perfectly fine signature—every bit as nice as Konerko's. The value of sports memorabilia derives from the outcomes achieved on the field, often the results of the energies expended throughout an entire career. It has nothing to do with the signature itself.

I did not know anything about Chris Burke before finding that ball. I am sure this is not the outcome he expected to create when signing it. Certainly he did not predict that it would eventually become one of the most prized possessions of a White Sox fan. Playing several years of Major League Baseball is no failure by any measure.

But every day when I sit down in my office to try to improve businesses with data, I see that ball perched on my desk. And every day it reminds me of an important lesson that guides everything that I do:

"Don't be Chris Burke"—meaning "Try Not to Accidentally Decrease Value Through My Actions Despite Having Good Intentions." This resolves to the convenient and easy-to-remember acronym TNADVTMADHGI. Or just remember "Don't be Chris Burke" and recall this story.

When we find ourselves in a Chris Burke-like situation, we should try to calibrate our behavior so we are more likely to create real value in the end. And if you are literally Chris Burke, sorry for using you as a cautionary tale in a data book, and thanks for the autograph!

Whether we are talking about ourselves or others, we are spending a lot of time talking about trying to change people's behaviors, while acknowledging that it is really challenging to change people's behavior. This is why Data Leadership hasn't really been addressed before in the way we are talking about it in this book: it is not about data at all—it is all about changing people's behavior.

MAKE-AN-IMPACT! We know a few truths about people:

1. People resist change.

2. People are watching out for themselves above all else.

3. Even if doing something would benefit themselves, see point #1.

Does that sound like a party we want to attend? Seems like a recipe for disaster, and that's exactly what happens when people try to do data by coming in guns a-blazing with a bunch of meetings alongside grandiose ambitions of changing everything! Of course it is doomed to failure—do we expect fundamental human nature to step aside just because data is important? Do we think we're going to make a difference by getting some people in a room to argue about who our customer is?

We need to be much more thoughtful on how we engage, especially in the early days. We must operate in the shadows of our organizations, doing good for the sake of doing good, and building capabilities that are useful immediately for people just trying to get their normal stuff done.

To be an effective Data Leader, we should take a page from the Agile world, where they have spent years trying to be more responsive than "traditional" waterfall project management methodologies allow. Though there is a lot of good throughout Agile, the point we want to highlight right now is a management philosophy called servant leadership.

Servant leadership is a term that actually is what it says it is (Data Management folks take note)! Servant leaders help their teams succeed by removing anything that blocks them from completing their tasks. Whether reaching out to the business for requirements clarifications, or procuring new technical tools, or jumping in to lend some specific expertise—servant leaders stop at nothing to support their teams. Data Leaders must approach our roles similarly.

MAKE-AN-IMPACT! Though we might not even have clearly defined teams, Data Leaders do have at least one shared goal with everyone we encounter, whether or not they know it: to create Data Value.

We must remove the blockers and help that value become realized.

It does not even need to be complicated. By leveraging the Simple Virtuous Cycle, it can be as easy as:

- Wake up.

- Create Data Value (Measure, Identify Improvements, Improve).

- Go to sleep, excited to do it again tomorrow!

But doesn't that oversimplify it a bit? Sure, but not as much as it might initially seem. We as people, especially those of us interested in data and technology, tend to overcomplicate things. The blockers we encounter may come from organizational resistance, a "not my job" mentality, fear of change, lack of technology tools, or good ol' laziness.

So what? We have already established that the futures of our businesses are on the line, and we are the keys that will unlock Data Value. If there were no blockers, people would have fixed all this already, and we wouldn't have such awesome opportunities in front of us. When faced with the incredible potential of transforming our businesses, none of the blockers out there should remain for long.

We understand what creates Data Value, how it is measured, and why trying to go too big initially is a recipe for disaster. If we look for the little ways to plug in our ability to create business outcome improvements, we will succeed.

If we are still feeling a little leery about stepping into the spotlight as a Data Leader, think about the worst case scenario: our passion about changing the world (or at least our businesses) with Data Value falls on completely deaf ears, and the rest of our company's leadership has no interest in improving business outcomes. Beyond not supporting us, they actually are so averse to challenging the status quo that they fire us. What happens then?

First, the chances of that are insanely low, but let's explore, since it is always a good idea to explore border conditions. There are far too many organizations out there desperately trying to find a way to use data better—do not waste your time with one that you need to convince that data is important. Today the idea of working for a data-ignorant company is like working for a company that refuses to let people access the internet. Do they still use paper ledgers for accounting too? Slide rules? Horse-drawn carriages?

The bottom line is that creating real Data Value is hard enough to get right in an organization that "gets it" and fully supports our data endeavors. Let's not waste our time working for those organizations that are already toast—and make no mistake, if they haven't figured out by now that data is valuable, they are already too far gone.

MAKE-AN-IMPACT! It is not too late for an organization that realizes data is valuable, wants to do something about it, but has no idea what to do—but there is no time left to waste.

The fact is that *most* organizations today find truth in the above statement, and there is certainly still hope for them. Especially since they have us.

PART 2: THE DATA LEADERSHIP FRAMEWORK

ACCESS giving people ways to interact with the data	REFINE optimizing potential data value (DV)
I. DATA SECURITY	I. METADATA
II. DATA ARCHITEC-TURE	II. DATA QUALITY
III. DATA WRANGLING	III. MASTER DATA
IV. DEVELOP-MENT	IV. ENRICH-MENT
V. SUPPORT OPS & DEV OPS	V. CURATION

The 25 DLF **DISCIPLINES** are input-oriented & actionable

POTENTIAL
DATA VALUE (DV)

ADOPT	IMPACT	ALIGN
realizing data value (DV) by putting it to use	maximizing business outcomes	engagement of all stakeholders
I. DATA MODELLING & WAREHOUSING	I. MEASUREMENTS METRICS & KPIs	I. STRATEGIES, STANDARDS & POLICIES
II. TRADITIONAL REPORTING	II. REGRESSION ANALYSIS & PREDICTIVE MODELING	II. PROJECT & PROGRAM MANAGEMENT
III. INTERACTIVE DASHBOARDS & VISUALIZATIONS	III. MACHINE LEARNING & ARTIFICIAL INTELLIGENCE	III. MARKETING & COMMUNI-CATIONS
IV. SYSTEMS INTEGRATION	IV. BUSINESS PROCESS AUTOMATION	IV. ORGANIZATIONAL TRAINING & BUILDING A QUANTITATIVE CULTURE
V. EMERGING DATA TECHNOLOGIES	V. DATA MONETIZATION	V. REGULATORY COMPLIANCE

$\mapsto$ ACTUAL DATA VALUE (DV) $\dashv$

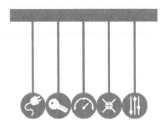

6 INTRODUCING THE DATA LEADERSHIP FRAMEWORK

We attend Data Management conferences, and find no executives. We attend technology conferences, and find no data people. Executives have their own secret conferences somewhere only for them. This is no surprise, as there is nothing more human than breaking ourselves off into little groups to talk about stuff.

We've spent decades breaking our companies into subsets of functional expertise, and we have reinforced these divisions by disincentivizing folks from working together. For most corporate positions, our compensation structures tend to focus on our individual activities instead of the actual impact we have on the business. How many bonuses are determined by how well the technology team impacted operational efficiencies? Too few.

This isn't because we want our people to have minimal impact on the business with what they do all day—it is because measuring that contribution is hard. And if measuring it is hard, then creating incentives around it is harder, and then coaching folks' behaviors to make it happen becomes downright dismal. We'd rather just tell people to knock out some widgets and call it a day.

Fortunately, the intrepid Data Leader will not back down from this kind of challenge. We recognize that the more difficult path will lead us to our greater potential, and that the pain of creating better incentive structures is just one of the many side effects of transforming our businesses to become data-driven. It's like exercise: we may feel sore after a workout, but we know inside that what we did will ultimately be good for our health.

Organizational healthiness sounds like it would be a great idea to shoot for, but it is a nebulous metric to define. Which numbers would go into that? Plenty of companies make tremendous profit, but so did Sears, until it didn't. Growth could be another subcomponent, but then you look back at a company like Enron, which had a trajectory like the model rocket I built in high school that I strapped eight extra engines onto. My rocket was also remarkably fast, largely unstable, and caused a bit of a fire when it crashed.

For us, it all comes back to Data Value. If we are using data to create real differentials in business outcomes, then hopefully we are on the right track. Can data be used to manipulate the perceived impacts, or show positive net gains when the reality is far worse? Of course. There's also data that, if analyzed properly, will help us uncover any misleading conclusions.

The Data Leadership Framework was born from this premise, and from observing the rampant ineffectiveness of data efforts currently existing in many of our organizations. These efforts are often incomplete, overly subjective, or completely miss some important aspect that if addressed, would lead to much better outcomes. Companies' typical project-based change management approach amplifies these problems. With finite timelines, resources, and scope, we compromise our ability to react to new information without laborious change requests or approval processes—if we are lucky enough to gain approval at all. The net result to the project deliverables is cutting corners on things like testing, design, or robustness of the solution—but there is another hidden drawback that is even worse.

MAKE-AN-IMPACT! If we optimize energies solely at the micro-scale (the project), we lose the ability to maximize impacts at the macro-scale (the system).

This means that absent well-coordinated Data Governance and Project/Program Management, our collections of individual projects will not result in the transformative impacts they were intended to have. It's as if we spent all of our time polishing grains of sand and then were surprised to learn that we had not created a beach, but instead we had created a desert.

While there are countless resources out there to help us get better at individual Data Management disciplines, there is a startling lack of resources to help us put them all together. The Data Leadership Framework is designed to help us keep an eye on the overall transformative impact we're having, and to help us correct course before we waste a ton of effort building something amazing in the wrong place. Context is what makes data useful, and the Data Leadership Framework provides much-needed macro-scale context to the detailed activities we spend most of our time doing.

Similarly, there is even more written on building great businesses and developing leadership skills—but where's the beef? These leadership-focused works often fail to connect us to the daily grind of things like projects, operations, budgets, priorities, and varied expectations of stakeholders. People are trying to lead businesses at a time when data is crucial to success, but still do not grasp foundational Data Management principles that are more important now than ever!

The data-oriented professional who wants to be successful must recognize that their fate is either to become a business leader, or risk becoming irrelevant. Data Leadership is really all about organizational change—which implies that the people involved will need to do something different. And this is true in the case of Data Value—until somebody takes action, any data-driven insights may be interesting, but have only created potential value.

Data Management seems much easier for us to fall back on—we can actually control the data! The downside is that we won't really accomplish much until we connect the data capabilities to people. Changing people's behavior doesn't work like putting data through an ETL (Extract-Transform-Load) process. Though some ETL processes are less manageable than a child trying to avoid bedtime, most ETL processes do what they're told.

MAKE-AN-IMPACT! Data folks love building data capabilities, and may act like other people get in the way—but people are the main way data realizes its potential value.

We're just going to have to accept that to create Data Value we need to address both the data and people sides of the equation, and we might as well throw in technology and process sides, too. If you think of data and people as the nouns, and technology and process as the verbs, these are the underpinnings of the entire Data Leadership Framework (DLF). We use a data-focused nomenclature in the DLF, but everything can be further distilled into people, process, data, and technology elements.

MAKE-AN-IMPACT! The Data Leadership Framework helps us achieve balance between the people, process, technology, and data capabilities we must create to maximize Data Value.

First we break down the universe of things we care about in data into five DLF Categories: Access, Refine, Adopt, Impact, and Align. Each of these have a distinct and significant role, and with a balanced approach to address all of them we will be able to create realized Data Value. The underlying hypothesis is that for the system to operate most effectively, these five categories must be in relative balance—that is, their overall output capacity must be of comparable strength to one another.

Within each of these DLF Categories we have five disciplines representing data and organizational change management functions where we can choose to devote energy (in the form of time, money, attention, etc.). The five DLF Disciplines in each DLF Category do not need to be balanced within an individual category, but the disciplines should be used to compare and prioritize the allocation of finite resources toward the categorically-aligned goal.

This will become clearer as we progress through the categories and disciplines, but for now know that the DLF Categories are outcome-oriented, and the DLF Disciplines are input-oriented. We cannot, for example, simply say we want to devote more resources to the DLF Refinement capabilities without at some point allocating them to specific efforts in Data Quality, Metadata, etc.

MAKE-AN-IMPACT! DLF Disciplines are actionable, whereas the DLF Categories represent the generalized results of those actions.

Another way to think about it is that the DLF Categories are the conceptual-level that typically resonates with business stakeholders. DLF Disciplines are more Data Management-specific, but also necessarily the level of insight we need to get to if we want to know what to do next. This brings up a good professional tip: always aim to know at least one more level of detail than the questions you expect to receive. It not only ensures you have the requisite mastery of a subject, but it also gives you the ability to answer questions confidently. There is a difference!

MAKE-AN-IMPACT! The DLF is designed to be an aid in assessing existing environments, developing strategic approaches, and most importantly, helping us know what to do next.

Before we get into the specifics of the DLF, it's also important to understand that the DLF is a framework. It is intended to make complex subjects simpler for us to evaluate, prioritize, and compare with one another. The DLF does not contain specific answers so much as it helps us ask the right questions to determine what we need to do to create Data Value in our particular context. It is most simply a starting point—one which we are all encouraged to use, adapt, and evolve to meet the needs of our individual organizations.

Just like few folks can find perfectly fitting formalwear off the rack, most companies will need some DLF-tailoring before it fits like a glove. Whether adjusting some of the terminology, breaking it out into more or fewer components, or removing or recasting some parts entirely, it's all fair game. We're doing it, too! If we let maximizing Data Value be our guide, nothing is off limits. But before running off to change it, let's first spend some time understanding what the Data Leadership Framework is—and that it represents the knowledge gained from decades of professional experience maximizing Data Value.

As we dive into the details, remember that each category overall, and each discipline within them, individually creates potential value. The category with the lowest Data Value creation capability limits the overall system's potential throughput. To create the category-level balance it is reasonable to invest more or less energy in individual disciplines, even omitting some entirely at times.

Category-level balance is almost always achieved through a wildly varying approach across DLF Disciplines. Since every organization has some things they do well, and others they do not do well, the right allocation of energy to disciplines will depend much on that. Addition-ally, over time the allocations will change as new capabilities are introduced, and the efforts necessary to maintain these capabilities are lesser than that what it took to build them initially.

MAKE-AN-IMPACT! Data Leaders strive to understand an entity's capabilities across the DLF Categories and Disciplines, guiding the prioritization and allocation of finite resources to maximize overall system balance and throughput.

Keep this mission in mind as we dive into the specifics, and remember that this is just the beginning. Each of the DLF Disciplines represents a subject area where people devote entire careers. There are certainly plenty of additional resources to learn more, and we should try to gain, at minimum, a foundational understanding in each of them. The upcoming chapters are a start, but represent more of a guide of what to study rather than enough depth to give us an fully-informed perspective on their own.

7 DLF ACCESS: PREPARE DATA FOR USE

It all starts with Data Access. Before we can create amazing capabilities that transform our businesses with Data Value, we need to connect to some data. This data can be sourced from countless places, both internal and external to our own organizations, using a variety of different technologies to facilitate these connections.

Typically, the most useful data for an organization to analyze is that which it creates directly through business operations. There are orders and transaction information, customer account records, products, part numbers, vendors, accounting journal entries, financial statements, HR and personnel information records—and these are just some obvious ones. Think about other things, like contracts, office leases, equipment, vehicles, insurance policies, compliance reports, and proprietary formulas and other trade secrets.

On top of those we can add things like social media feeds, system logs, machinery sensors, graphical information systems (location-based) data, RFIDs, and I'm pretty sure that those fancy door sensors that open with the cards create data, too. The point is that we have a *ton* of data, and we still haven't gone beyond the data created inside our own companies!

 MAKE-AN-IMPACT! The fact is that most organizations manage to mess up internal data so badly that they never reach the point where they should go looking for data from the outside.

We will not suffer this fate. Using the Data Leadership Framework, we will be able to manage all of the data we can find—and we will always be hungry for more!

These are unprecedented times, after all. The world of data has never been more complex, with unbelievably capable technology tools and massive volumes larger than anything in the history of the world! The challenges we face as data professionals are so incredibly varied and expansive that it is monumentally difficult simply keeping up with the rapid pace of technology innovations that are enabling ever more data to be created and consumed!

And it will never be easier than it is right now.

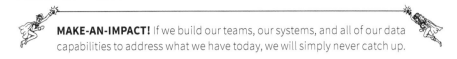

By the time we are capable of satisfying what we know we need right now, the world will change around us. The target will move, and we will still be behind where we need to be. This is why we must build extensible systems that can be adapted quickly to whatever the future may bring.

We do not have to predict the exact future to have systems that will accommodate it. We know the data will become more complex. Bigger. Faster. With new kinds of ever-more-granular precision, with businesses and potentially entire industries being built on organizations' ability to act quickly on aggregations and patterns that today we cannot even identify. Cryptocurrencies, blockchains, self-driving cars—this stuff is going to continue to evolve, and it is only getting faster—and if this stuff doesn't get us excited about a career in data, we are in the wrong line of work!

Before we get too far ahead of ourselves, as we mentioned at the start of this section, it all starts with Data Access. And in the Data Leadership Framework, Access starts with Security. In today's world, anything we do with data must be done with an eye to appropriate use, privacy, and being good shepherds of the power data contains. By starting our journey with Data Security, it reminds us of these responsibilities, and gives us the appropriate context for the capabilities we build.

 ## *Data Security*

We're kicking things off with an area that tends to be hyper-focused on by people who specialize in it, and largely ignored by those who do not. This has to change, since security risks are only becoming higher and higher profile. The 2017 Equifax breach settled this debate. When one of the pillars of the U.S. system of financial trust (i.e., personal credit) is compromised, and then their leadership bungles their response so spectacularly, the one thing we should immediately realize is that we never want that to be our company.

We won't even discuss the casino that got hacked through a smart fish tank feeding system. Yes, that really happened.*

Data Security ensures that people have access to the information that they should, and people who should not have access, don't. Beyond that, security processes must reduce the likelihood that information is unintentionally shared with people it should not be. These people may be bad actors, trying to break into data systems. It may also be the general public, just hanging out waiting for data to be dumped into their laps.

Security efforts, not unlike most Data Management functions, tend to be motivated by a few common patterns:

- A breach or other catastrophe has already occurred.

- A regulatory/compliance/audit finding has identified non-conformance or a lack of competency.

- An executive read something that got them worked up. This is a surprisingly frequent cause of major corporate initiatives.

- A well-reasoned business strategy has recognized that valuable data assets should be treated appropriately.

It may be clear by the wording, but my preference is that we want to be strategically-motivated to do these things—but in real-world circumstances, the preceding list is ordered from most-likely to least-likely in what will bring Security to the top of your to-do list.

Recall that the Data Leadership Framework has five different categories composed of 25 different disciplines to think about and balance our meager resources across. Each of them is going to feel important when we think about them in detail. We must do our best to figure out at any moment in time which ones are going to help balance the categories and create the most realized Data Value in the end.

Data Security is especially interesting when put in this context. When we consider the three forces of Data Value (increase revenue, decrease costs, manage risks), Data Security is going to primarily help manage risk. If we do Security well, we will probably avoid losing a lot of money due to not having it—but we still might even then. Certainly we do not want to do Data Security at the expense of everything else in the DLF, but if we don't at least establish some core capabilities we will be incurring an outsized amount of unnecessary risk.

Not quite a bumper-sticker-ready sales pitch, is it?

It's inconvenient and annoying to have to deal with Security. This is why nobody likes the CISO (Chief Information Security Officer). Always running about, talking how the sky is falling and we are all doomed. That is a tough life. It's not that what the CISO says is wrong or unimportant (we just explained why it is super-important, in fact)—it is just that CISOs often present one-sided arguments about what we *shouldn't* do, or *can't* do, or *aren't allowed* to do without considering that businesses don't become successful solely by not doing things.

MAKE-AN-IMPACT! Organizations must balance their value-creating activities with negative-value-avoiding activities to end up with the most Data Value.

This brings us back to us. We need to be mindful of Data Security constraints as we develop all of the other capabilities to create Data Value. These seemingly-opposed forces are hard for us to do full justice to—as they require fundamentally different mindsets. Now if only we could find an ally who would help propel our Data Leadership efforts with Security. Perhaps it may be someone having trouble connecting their work to business value, and may be under-appreciated in the organization.

Aha! We could help the CISO (or equivalent position in the organization)! If nobody like that exists, we could build a business case for getting somebody doing that role. If an organization fights the need for Data Security after Equifax (or that fish-tank casino story), we have big problems! If I found myself in that situation, I'd appeal directly to the CEO—but if that didn't work, it might be time to find new employment at an organization that wants to survive in today's data-driven world.

But sadly, simply deciding to invest some energy in Data Security is not an impressive win. We have not actually done anything to build Data Security yet. Data Security may reasonably start with identifying particular areas of risk, crafting some policies, establishing acceptable uses, and getting some people to agree that those are good ideas.

Again, good talking about important things, but nothing real has happened.

We then need to implement the ideas. Our new friend the CISO, with additional support from others in IT, plus buy-in from the business (with a willingness to change some of their ways for the benefits of safety), a bit of time, plus ability to bridge any skills gaps, which there always are—if we can do all of these things, we can begin to implement some functional security capabilities that will help us manage data-related risk in our business.

Seems like a lot of work, right? Yeah, it is. All of this is a lot of work. It will be easy to burn out our team or wear out our welcome if we're not careful.

As we move into review of other disciplines and the need to maintain balance throughout the categories, the following is a good rule of thumb to follow:

MAKE-AN-IMPACT! In the beginning of our Data Leadership journey, we should do a little of many things, a lot of a few things, and one thing to become world-class. This becomes a promise of what is possible. Becoming excellent at one thing is the way to build confidence that we can become great at anything.

Data Security is probably an essential place to spend some time, but it is probably not the place most of us should try to become world-class (apologies to the CISOs out there). A risk mitigation Data Value dynamic is not strong enough to prioritize Security over other Data Leadership disciplines. That being the rule, of course there are exceptions.

If we are in the credit-reporting business or some other industry of such high trust where a data breach would likely result in bankruptcy, Data Security may well be the place to become world-class. Consumer-facing financial institutions, healthcare-related organizations with private health information (PHI), or defense-related companies may well have Security at or near the top of their priorities. With regulatory developments like HIPAA and the European GDPR (General Data Protection Regulation), the stakes are getting ever-higher.

Data Security competency is essential for all businesses. But doing it alone at the expense of all the other Data Leadership disciplines would be just as egregious. There is nothing to protect if our businesses fail because they could not use data to improve revenue and reduce expenses. Balance, baby. It's everything.

 Data Architecture

Data Architecture has become an interesting term these days. It used to be *relatively* simple (get it?), because at the center of everything we had a big relational Data Warehouse where we would have a Data Model that reflected a refactoring of the contents of various data sources to create a form that is generally intuitive for a wide variety of data consumers. Wait—that's not simple! Let's try that again:

Data Architecture used to be simpler than it is today because the Data Warehouse dominated much of the conversation, specifically after the operational systems created the data. Today, because data has become so central to business operations, the Data Architecture discipline has grown to cover more ground.

Data Architecture now has moved closer to more traditional Enterprise Architecture. Technology systems are all data-driven, and a Data Architect needs to curate information flows in much more dynamic ways than back in the olden times of the early 2000s. We are far removed from the days of taking a few data sources, modeling them into a dimensional model, knocking out some ETL, and then hitting the golf course. Today's Data Architects have visibility and responsibility across much of the organization.

Not only are the systems that create and use data becoming more complex, but today's data consumers are also more sophisticated; they are developing regression analysis and predictive analytics, or demanding real-time interactive dashboards that are device-agnostic.

 MAKE-AN-IMPACT! The tools we have now can handle an incredible amount of data throughput, and it is up to us to fill those pipes with good stuff!

Fortunately, the data providers and sourcing options are just as plentiful. Many organizations have become data services providers, happily willing to provide us whatever we can imagine, for a fee. Even for us cheapskates, there are a tremendous number of free and open data sources available. If you want to do something like weather-trend sales analysis, the amount of free weather data available out there will blow your mind!

So we've covered the bookends of data consumers and producers, but what about all of the operational systems inside our businesses? All of those internally created data sources we talked about earlier are also driven and enhanced by data. The Data Architects need to get these systems to play nicely to share their information effectively—all the while acting in accordance with Data Governance and Security policies. So there are smaller data feedback loops that get created to serve operational processes within the overall Data Value chain—and Data Architects are involved with it all!

 MAKE-AN-IMPACT! Data Architecture is no longer just about the relational Data Warehouse that needs to serve up information to some analysts. Data Architecture is everywhere throughout our businesses.

It's the Data Architects who weave this tapestry of capabilities together and ensure that the data can flow as needed. Frankly, in addition to the substantial amount of work in Data Architecture alone, most Data Architects get pulled into a dozen other roles covered by the Data Leadership Framework.

So where does Data Architecture fit in? Well, everybody needs at least a little bit to make anything work with Data Value, so it has to be on the radar and get some attention. The funny thing is that we probably have a lot of it already—it just may have been built haphazardly with no coordination and is now causing a bunch of problems with sharing information.

Sounds a lot like Data Governance when we think about it. The fact is that Data Architecture *is* a lot like Data Governance in that both disciplines create structures and processes for information to flow. The difference is that Data Governance does it with a focus on the people impacting the data flows through business process, and Data Architecture concerns itself more with the technology systems and databases that impact the physical data movements and storage.

The wrong way of thinking about these disciplines is to plan on, for example, doing a big, isolated Data Architecture project to give that area a boost. It may be more appropriate to think of these disciplines as lenses that allow us to see specific aspects of truth. Even better, if you think of the Data Leadership disciplines as differently colored lights that, when combined, illuminate truth without bias—that may be the closest to what we are trying to achieve.

Regardless of our preferred analogy, Data Architecture is a deep bucket, and because it is influenced so much by technology, it changes constantly. Data Architects will know relational databases and be fluent in SQL, pretty much always. If a Data Architect doesn't at least know SQL, it is going to be difficult to be good at the job. SQL skills are necessary but insufficient to become exceptional at Data Architecture.

MAKE-AN-IMPACT! Great Data Architects understand how the business will derive realized value from data.

They will not necessarily need to have deep, heartfelt conversations directly with the business on a regular basis, but they will need to be able to grasp the business enough to make independent and accurate determinations about design and technology. We cannot afford to slow down the process by spoon-feeding Data Architects everything they need to take into account to design what needs to be done.

Finally, Data Architects must be self-motivated and push to get things built at all costs. Passive Data Architects are going to fail us every time. If we are performing the Data Architecture role ourselves, that may be a good strategy—but we must recognize that we will need some extra help on the business or technical sides if our responsibilities spread across many other Data Leadership disciplines.

Data Architecture is no doubt an important consideration in any organization, but like many other design activities, it has a tendency to fall into the "talking about working" trap. If we have some foundational Data Architecture directives in place, that may be all we need to start getting our hands dirty and start building our data-driven future. And nothing dirties the hands quite like Data Wrangling.

 ## *Data Wrangling*

"Data Wrangling" as a name chosen to describe something in the Data Management space is about as good as it gets: action-oriented, describes what it actually does, and doesn't make people depressed as soon as they hear it. Data Wrangling is what you think it is— *wrastlin'* that there data into a place where we can control it! In case *wrastlin'* isn't a familiar term, it is like wrestling, but involves more mud and muck. And that's exactly how Data Wrangling feels!

Before there is a highly-refined Data Model, supporting architecture, and a corresponding process that helps folks who know what to do with it all, we have to figure some things out. Data Wrangling is all about early-stage data preparation where we get it somewhere we can use it before we decide if it is worth putting it somewhere more robust.

MAKE-AN-IMPACT! Data Wrangling involves identifying potential data use cases, identifying source(s) of data to support them, and mocking up prototypes to see if our hypotheses have merit.

This sounds a lot like Data Science—and that is because data scientists often spend too much of their time doing Data Wrangling. Preparing data for use is generally a lower-value-added activity than performing fancy analyses, which is what data scientists should be spending most of their time doing. If we want to get the most out of our Data Science investments, we should teach the data to walk before the scientists make it dance later.

So Data Wrangling is about taking relatively ambiguous ideas about potential Data Value, and then doing a rough-cut of what might eventually evolve into a production solution. This is a departure from how they did things in old-world data shops, where everything is predetermined before anybody has a chance to learn anything from the development process itself.

It used to be that data projects were always done using a waterfall project management methodology. This gave false comfort to the people paying for the project, because so many of the details were laid out from the beginning. The problem is that so much of our knowledge and understanding, and in-turn optimal decision-making, is dependent on other things we know. Waterfall projects incorrectly imply that all relevant information is known during the design phase, but the truth is that we learn new things constantly throughout a project. Those new learnings should be applied to drive optimal designs and decisions for the rest of the project, and waterfall methodologies only accommodate in-flight changes through friction-heavy change requests and refactoring processes.

MAKE-AN-IMPACT! Waterfall data projects can move in any direction you want, as long as you want everything to come crashing down!

Data Wrangling is antithetical to waterfall project methodologies. Data Wrangling is a discovery process with a high degree of uncertainty, and will propel learning and movement in ways that cannot be easily predicted. Sure, we could conceivably wrap all this in a waterfall project, but why would we if the project management methodology adds nothing to help the actual work succeed? Then it becomes overhead for the sake of overhead, and this is not something we data professionals should be advocating that we do.

That said, the tools of Data Wrangling are as varied as data itself. When I am working on new data sourcing, my preference is to read file specs, try to view in a text editor (if applicable, and if the data file is small enough), or load it into a relational database. For very large files, data profiling tools that work at large scale can be helpful. Other data sources like streaming can require different tools and techniques. Python and microservices have enabled entirely new ways of processing data. Though the tools are incredibly varied, it largely depends on our personal technical proclivities and the types of data we are looking at.

Once we select the technologies we want to work with, we need to (for lack of a better term) play with the data. See if the data reflects its specifications (typically documentation is low on developers' priority lists). Figure out how we might join it to our existing data, and what path it might take to achieve the Data Value use cases we have in mind.

Data Wrangling is equal parts design and tinkering. It does not have a lot of prescribed activities, but it should result in a better understanding of what it will take to develop a more complete solution that will have a positive ROI. I like to think of Data Wrangling as a loose collection of mini-proofs-of-concept that will help us figure out the costs and benefits of particular options while minimizing the costs of doing that research.

MAKE-AN-IMPACT! Data Wrangling as a Data Leadership Framework Discipline is like investing in Research and Development: spending some energy here will lead to improvements and efficiencies throughout everything else we do.

Data Wrangling, when done effectively, will have a strong value proposition in the risk management area. It also may contribute to revenue increases by identifying new opportunities, and decreasing costs by informing better development approaches to avoid unnecessary mistakes and rework. Many times the techniques we prototype in the Data Wrangling area make it into the final projects.

I like doing Data Wrangling, myself. I find it an essential part of the design and architecture process. Just like a chef might want to touch and taste their ingredients, or visit the place from which their ingredients came, Data Leaders will want to get close to the sources of data. Remember, many data sources are internally-grown—so the above statement implies that Data Leaders will need to get close to the operations of their own organization. This means the systems, sure, but also the people and processes that are involved.

Later on we will try to influence these systems, people, and processes—but right now we just want to understand them. Will we ever have credibility in suggesting that things be done differently if we have not fully learned how they are done now? If we do not understand how things are done, will we have a hope of identifying why they are being done this way? The answer to both of those questions is "No." Sorry, rhetorical questions bother me.

Data Wrangling in many ways is a more tactical instantiation of Data Leadership as a whole. Data Leadership is not simply about achieving a Zen-like balance across Data Management topics. If we cast the light from each of the Data Leadership Disciplines at the problem, we will illuminate what we need to do to improve.

MAKE-AN-IMPACT! Data Leadership is about going down the road less traveled: the sources of the data pain in our organizations are likely found in areas of the Data Leadership Framework where the least energy is being expended.

Fixing them all, on the other hand, is a bigger challenge. It is a start to know what each of the disciplines are, what they do to promote Data Value, and how they relate to one another —but as we've mentioned before, this just scratches the surface of any individual topic.

With Data Leadership in general, and Data Wrangling in particular, the most important thing to do is start doing it. Be inquisitive, solve problems, break through the walls ourselves. If we are starting out in the smallest or most inexperienced environment, a little Data Security, a little Data Wrangling, and a little bit of insight about what data might help change for the better—these alone might be enough to move the needle and get your data efforts going.

That is another important lesson: Do not expect to be good at it all, or, especially in the early days, to even get to it all. In the world of data, we might have more blind spots than we do proficiencies, and that is okay. Only a fool would think they can handle all of these on their own. What we need to do is be realistic about what we are working with, and not extend past the breaking point. That said, we will absolutely need to push past the comfortable point. Data Leadership is all about pushing ourselves and our organizations beyond where we are comfortable—because that is why we are behind in the first place!

To do that, we're going to need to build something. That's when Development kicks in.

 ## *Development*

One of the most difficult things about being in a small business is that we never quite know where the breaking point is—and we become so accustomed to wearing different hats that we think we can wear every hat, all the time. This is often because, though we sure would like to hire experts to do everything, resources are limited and our spending priorities gravitate more toward electricity for the office and paying the salaries of the people we do have.

I once determined that the ETL tools that were available to me (for free) were subpar, and that I could do better. So I spent several months building my own ETL tool, using technologies I'd never used, with very high expectations for myself. I pushed hard day and night, and managed to create something objectively impressive in a short amount of time—with very limited assistance. It was one of the most frustrating, yet invigorating, periods in my career. I later got some help from a more practiced developer to smooth some of the rough edges, but it remained my design. It took a little doing, but we managed to get it in production for a client, and it is still running for them today.

Looking back on it, I'm not entirely sure whether this is an inspirational tale about following your ridiculous dreams to do something you probably shouldn't—or whether this is a cautionary warning that these ideas are ridiculous and you should perhaps be a little more careful with your ambition and time. Regardless, at some point in working with data we are going to need to build something that does not yet exist.

This is Data Development. The stakes are higher than for Data Wrangling, because we necessarily have higher expectations. This is where Data Value is born! Through the data capabilities we build, we give our businesses the connection to data-driven improvement opportunities.

 MAKE-AN-IMPACT! When we do Data Development, we should have already proven through Data Wrangling that our Data Value use cases are achievable, and we now are going to build out the full capability set with the intention of putting it into a production capacity for the organization.

Think about the interplay here between Data Development, Wrangling, and Architecture. Architecture informs the biggest brush-strokes, including the technologies we will use and the overall design integration. Data Wrangling proves out the smallest details, ensuring that we have the component pieces of data and process that we will ultimately need to have figured out. Data Development is where we actually build our future.

While too often we start as a Data Development team of one, most of the time we will need help to build the capabilities we need. A starting development team of two or three is more common and more useful, as people tend to gravitate to different specialties. We can loosely break these roles down between front-end (UI/UX), back-end (integration), and database (modeling and performance).

Our front-end, UI/UX (User-Interface/User-Experience) folks enjoy building what people see and interact with. They have a knack for designing what is pleasant to the eyes. These folks can build websites and applications, and are great to help with building dashboards and interactive reporting solutions. They can often lend a hand with our marketing efforts, especially in the early days. Later on, we can specialize further with developers and designers, but when starting out we will be happy if we have anybody who loosely fits this role.

The back-end integration specialists are the salt of the earth. With tools like Java, Python, and C++ (for the hard-core), these are the folks who unite the pretty things with the power of databases. They build out business logic through applications, connecting to APIs (Application Programming Interfaces), and generally solving problems and making stuff work however they can. Back-end developers are likely to be the ones trumpeting the cloud, microservices architectures, and serverless infrastructure. They also tend to champion open source, laptop stickers, and free t-shirts. If you can only bring one developer to your efforts, it probably needs to be somebody who identifies as part of this back-end integration specialist group, but can fake-it-till-they-make-it on front-end and database work.

Finally, database specialists are the heavy machinery operators of the bunch. Good ones have expanded their horizons to move beyond the monolithic relational databases, and see the value in new technologies—helping to bridge the knowledge gap between traditional data storage and warehousing and back-end application developers. Old-school database people are implanted with microchips that cause them to deny the existence of new database technologies like graph, NoSQL, and blockchain. Regardless, database folks must build out the systems that house billions of data records, serving up information to a myriad of system and human endpoints—it takes a unique set of skills and compulsion to be great at this stuff.

Things only get more complex from here. We can have entire teams dedicated to each of these functions—in fact, larger organizations will have entire teams dedicated to PARTS of these functions.

As you might imagine, coordinating efforts among all of these folks can take some serious energy of its own. Fortunately, there's a Data Leadership Framework Discipline for that! Admittedly, that is not quite as catchy as "there's an app for that!"—but we also don't have Apple's marketing budget. In fact, we should be happy that we have a catchphrase at all. Most data books don't even have that!

MAKE-AN-IMPACT! Development is a big topic by itself, just like all of the Data Leadership Framework Disciplines. Don't be afraid to start, but do be afraid to try to do it all on your own.

The next DLF Discipline expands upon what we've built in this chapter, as we focus on how to take what we've developed and nurture it to consistently deliver the most ongoing benefit. And do remember that we are still squarely in the "Access" category—simply trying to give people ways to interact with data that exists. Just wait until we *really* start using data to drive business impacts!

Support, Operations, and DevOps

This may look like a catch-all bucket, but don't let looks deceive you! Actually, in this case, looks are dead-on accurate because this is a catch-all bucket. What we don't want to do is think a catch-all bucket is less important.

The best Data Security, Data Architecture, Data Wrangling, and Data Development efforts will quickly become useless if we fail to establish appropriate processes around them. And before we get too far, note that this Support, Operations, and DevOps DLF Discipline is not the same as the Project and Program Management one we will cover in the Alignment category.

What we care about here is developing productive, data-focused, operational structures to manage ongoing data-related services, *within* the data endeavors themselves. In contrast to the Align category, which focuses on the engagement of the business, here we are being more introspective about the operations of our data folks.

MAKE-AN-IMPACT! We have to get our internal teams humming before we can reasonably hope to evolve the rest of our companies.

While data people need to be given ongoing attention and new challenges to be fulfilled and satisfied in their career, data itself works similarly—but instead of career satisfaction, data must be nurtured to drive meaningful business outcomes.

Think of data having a career ambition of creating as much Data Value as it can. It goes to work, sitting in its database table, hoping one day to serve in the SQL query of its dreams. Occasionally it is called upon, and the data performs its duties with vigor and aplomb. But what if the data is treated poorly, stored in underpowered databases with poorly-defined Data Models and lacking indexes and simple Metadata Management? In this case, data responds slowly, with timeouts and data quality issues much more likely to occur.

People and data, we're not so different after all.

MAKE-AN-IMPACT! The idea of being "done" with data is like being "done" with Human Resources—it is not going to happen.

This is what this whole DLF Discipline is about: giving data the ongoing nurturing it needs to perform once the initial project is over. We can't assume that data will be fine if left alone. It will decay and perform poorly when we need it.

So let's break it down a bit:

- **Support** is how we respond to others who need us to help them. This often comes in the form of emails or phone requests to fix something that is broken, or build some capability that doesn't already exist. We probably need to track these requests, their resolutions, and provide a mechanism to convert the bigger requests into projects. In smaller shops, the formality is probably going to be lesser, since we would often find ourselves spending time just recategorizing things that we will ultimately have to fix ourselves, anyway. In larger environments, we may have access to a support team, which will provide a front line to receive and document requests, and our higher-level folks can focus a greater percentage of their time on solving more challenging problems.

- **Operations** is how our teams function in going about our business. Data teams can be a bit funky, since we will have highly technical (sometimes highly specialized) people who will need to play nicely with far-less-technical business subject matter experts. Throw in project managers, business analysts, data scientists and analysts—and we have quite the motley crew. Especially when we think about how many data-centric folks have chosen this career due to their preference for talking with machines rather than people (no judgment here—I'm with you!). But add to all of this that many folks will have "day jobs" above and beyond their participation in our data endeavors, and we have a big challenge in front of us.

- **DevOps** is a scary term that we threw in so that you knew we were serious about this stuff! Actually, DevOps is part Development, and part Operations (another great term!), with the intent to maintain a better chain of custody for data responsibilities. This is why I started with a joke, as this topic gets a bit heavy. In short, if we have to support and operate what we build, we will be motivated to build things better. This can be particularly true in the data space because the interdependencies are abundant.

Hopefully the above descriptions help make sense of our catch-all bucket, and hopefully begin to make the case that these should be considered carefully and given an appropriate amount of attention if we want our data efforts to be sustainable in the long-term.

 MAKE-AN-IMPACT! Support, Operations, and DevOps is an area, like Data Governance, where we should expect each hypothetical dollar of investment to be returned to the organization at least three times over in productivity enhancements.

A minimum 3x return-on-investment is a rule of thumb that executives often use to quickly sort projects possibly worth attention versus those that are not. The thinking is that people are generally too optimistic, so when they claim 3x, a 2x return is a more probable outcome in the real world. Resources are scarce, and the disruptive nature of any significant change should at least double the amount of investment in return—whereas anything lower than a 2x return can be accomplished by less risky investments. It's this kind of thinking we need to be ready to overcome if we want our productivity improvement efforts to be seen as good investments.

So much of the rest of the Data Leadership Framework is about the business implications of data—whether it be improving its usefulness or being used and eventually driving the differentials in business outcomes. The DLF Access Category skews technical because this is where the foundation is laid. To build great capabilities through the rest of the Data Leadership Framework, we must have sound technology fundamentals from which to support our lofty business-facing ambition.

Data Access is where it all begins. Where we can start working with data before we even know whether or not it will be of any value in the end. Where we can experiment at low risk and low costs, finding the best ideas from which to develop lasting solutions. Where data technologists can play with data from their home in the dark catacombs of our office buildings, where they won't scare the pretty people.

It's Data Access that is the doorway to the rest of the data capabilities we will build. Once the data is in house, we can accomplish anything! And we will—in the next chapter we look at the ways we turn data from the raw materials into the insights that will transform our organizations! Are we excited yet? Let's do this!

8 DLF REFINEMENT: OPTIMIZE DATA POTENTIAL

Data Refinement is where we focus on assessing and strategically improving our data so it fulfills the business impacts we have in mind. Our ability to create data-driven changes in business outcomes depends on this DLF Category.

 *Metadata*

If we want to create positive change, first we need to know where things stand now. This is fundamentally what Metadata Management is about. Data nerds who like being clever over being helpful define Metadata as "data about data." While this is technically true, people tend to ignore this definition as silly talk that makes no sense. This is also technically true, as recursive logic is often difficult for our human brains to understand.

Attempting to be both helpful and handsome, I prefer to define Metadata as "anything that provides context to data." Metadata tells the story of data, and that story can often be more useful than the data itself. Here's why:

4

That number four up there is data. Not very useful sitting around by itself, is it?

What if I told you that the number represents how many cookies each child will receive?

What if I told you that it was the number of days since we last had a fatal workplace accident?

What if I told you that it is just a number I chose to explain Metadata and then had to make up some other examples?

The context of the data matters. A lot. Perhaps your reaction when we were talking about cookies was "Heck, yeah! Cookie time!"—or it could have been "Hmm. Four cookies seems like a lot for a child. Should we really be advocating contributing to the childhood obesity epidemic?" The workplace accident example probably raised your level of attentiveness and caused a dozen additional questions to flood your mind. The final explanation, though actually correct in this example, seems like a waste of a good number four.

This exercise teaches us that a number four is not terribly interesting by itself. But hopefully it also illustrates that Metadata is pretty much everything we think about when we think that we are thinking about data. Yes, that is a lot of thinking, and that's why most people would prefer to ignore Metadata entirely, but now we know better!

Metadata comes in two basic flavors: Technical and Business. Technical Metadata is by far the most common, since every technology system creates Metadata of some sort. These can take the form of log files, databases, configuration settings, system reports—you name it. Technical Metadata is pretty easy to Access (pun intended!) and put somewhere where it can be used for Data Value purposes.

MAKE-AN-IMPACT! The downside of Technical Metadata is that it is so abundant that it has lots of worthless stuff in with the good—a low Data Value Density.

Yes, I do think we coined that term just now. Pretty exciting, eh? Data Value Density becomes an especially important consideration when we think about Big Data, but it applies in a lot of settings, including here with Metadata. The goal is to find relatively low-effort ways to compile data with high Data Value Density (like internal order data), before taking on high-effort activities that have low Data Value Density (like the Twitter firehose). Technical Metadata is a low Data Value Density asset that takes relatively little effort to compile—not the worst thing to spend a little time on, but we should temper expectations of what it will do for us.

In contrast, Business Metadata has a high Data Value Density. This is because, by definition, it has business relevance. This is Metadata that comes from people's brains. It can be conveyed through documentation, conversations, the Excel spreadsheets Bob put together— you name it. Business Metadata is so valuable because it cannot be created without people making a dedicated effort, and if that effort isn't made, the knowledge could be lost forever.

Let's consider one of the favorite activities of a Data Governance organization: compiling agreed-upon definitions of business terms into a Business Glossary. This is first and foremost a Metadata Management exercise. We are reaching into the business to identify Business Metadata, with a corresponding (Meta)Data Quality initiative to consolidate varied interpretations into coherent definitions that reflect the best available understanding of truth.

Another extension of Metadata is Data Lineage. Data Lineage is Metadata over time: it tells the life story of data as it is created, refined, aggregated, and used as part of a Data Value Proposition. Data Lineage can be a powerful tool to understand how a piece of information made it to a report we are viewing—and why two numbers that seem like they should match, don't.

MAKE-AN-IMPACT! Metadata Management describes the world around us. It provides a more complete understanding of our businesses today, so we can improve our businesses tomorrow.

One risk we can stumble into when taking on a Metadata-driven exercise is to jump too quickly into solutioning. For example, if Jim is giving us a definition of a customer, we might lead him by telling him Sally's definition. Jim will be inclined to anchor his response based on Sally's, and maybe even just agree entirely. We could have extracted some meaningful insights from variances in definitions—but instead we took a shortcut and missed an opportunity to do a better job. This happens all the time, and people usually have no idea they are making mistakes.

MAKE-AN-IMPACT! Data Leaders should advocate Judgment-Free Metadata Management. Do not impose what your view of truth should be, simply capture what is actually there.

We will have plenty of time to try to change the world later, but if we are working from a faulty map it will hurt those efforts down the road. The resources to teach us good Judgment-Free Metadata Management techniques may appear to be lacking, at least if we plug that specific term into a search box. Fortunately, there is an entire world of deep knowledge available that goes under another name: Marketing Research.

The Marketing Research field is enlightening in many ways, as the entire domain is about gathering information about opinions and preferences to better understand market opportunities. Two crucial areas for every Data Leader to study are how to conduct focus groups and how to write surveys. Be aware, however: once armed with this knowledge, there is no going back! It is a life of constant frustration to see how terribly most information-gathering exercises are performed.

Marketing folks are an incredible untapped data resource in many organizations. These people are often already doing more with data and analytics than almost anyone in our companies, and they understand ambiguity and how to use information with imperfect quality.

MAKE-AN-IMPACT! If we are fortunate enough to have a Marketing department, we should find some way to engage their talent in our Data Leadership efforts.

But for now, let's get back to Metadata, and specifically how we gather all this Metadata into a place where we can use it to drive Data Value. There are plenty of tools that help us collect Business Metadata, and countless ways to compile Technical Metadata. But to get started, we should pick our favorite spreadsheet program and track down interesting stories. By the time we hate our spreadsheet program we will know what we need from a more capable tool.

Just be warned, if we start with powerful tools before we've outgrown what we already have, we will not only waste money but we will miss out on important context. Tool shortcuts can be just as dangerous as process mistakes!

MAKE-AN-IMPACT! We should earn the tools we buy. Don't buy something because we might run into a wall without it. Wait until we can see the wall with enough clarity to realize that to get past it, we're going to need a bigger hammer.

So much is wasted on tools that are underutilized. Metadata Repository, Data Catalog, Data Dictionary, Data Lineage—these are all important functions that we need to think about. But getting somebody to swing a mediocre hammer is still going to accomplish more than even the greatest Thor-hammer sitting on a table with nobody picking it up.

Focus energy on motivating people first, and optimizing tools second. This helps us achieve more efficiency in our resource investments, and provides a valuable secondary benefit: we are able to learn and calibrate our activities in a smaller, safer context before we amplify them with more powerful tools. Since optics are important, we want to limit the blast radius of our mistakes while amplifying when we get it right.

Just like with a stereo speaker, any amplifier makes unwanted noise louder, too. That is, unless we can remove that noise. Hello, Data Quality!

 ## *Data Quality*

In contrast to Metadata Management, which is a complex term to describe relatively simple concepts, Data Quality is a seemingly simple term that actually confuses everybody. Because the words "data" and "quality" are familiar, people logically infer that we are talking about making data as good (i.e. high quality) as it can be. This is an incomplete and over-simplified understanding of what is actually a much more diverse subject.

In practice, this flawed notion of Data Quality has caused rampant data trust issues— because we have essentially set expectations that data needs to be perfect to be worth using. Not true! In absence of anything else, we certainly prefer higher-quality data to lower-quality data—but if our goal is to create maximum Data Value compared to the resources and energy expended, we need a better understanding of what Data Quality really is.

MAKE-AN-IMPACT! Data Quality is a discipline to assess and optimize data's suitability-for-use in Data Value-creating endeavors.

Let's break this down a little bit more:

- *"Data Quality is a discipline"* that we see everywhere in Data Management. Even if we disagree on the specifics of the definition, we can agree that Data Quality is pretty important.

- *"Assess and optimize data's suitability-for-use"* is the heart of it all. Data Quality is first about understanding the specific aspects of data that make it useful or not useful. This is an extension of Metadata Management, where we are now applying judgment to figure out whether the truth that exists is optimal for the actual demands we will place on the data to drive Data Value activities. Where it is suboptimal, we may strategically choose to apply additional energy to the data to improve its usefulness.

- *"In Data Value-creating endeavors"* implies that data will often have more than one use. We need to look at as many of them as we can and factor the collective needs into our prioritization.

And this is why understanding this Data Quality definition is so important:

MAKE-AN-IMPACT! When we take the time to understand which data will drive value, how much value we estimate that to be, and what the suitability characteristics of that data are—then we can actually prioritize our Data Quality efforts!

The alternative is haphazardly applying resources allocated to Data Quality in the hopeless pursuit of perfection, typically in response to whoever is complaining loudest. So how does this work?

- We must first figure out where the data in question falls on this Data Quality suitability-for-use spectrum, and apply a scoring methodology that will be meaningful to those who will use it.

- The best approach is to start simple to articulate basic usefulness, and then iterate through the more complex aspects that determine suitability for our organization's needs.

- Then we will communicate these characteristics of the data to the folks who need it.

MAKE-AN-IMPACT! If we want Data Quality to play a meaningful role in our organizations, a suitability-for-use assessment should be provided alongside any data used to drive business outcomes.

When is the last time we saw a suitability-for-use assessment accompanying data in a report or application? "Never" is sadly the most likely answer. A suitability-for-use assessment, often distilled into a Data Quality Score, can be as thorough or simple as the situation warrants. Like so many of the Data Leadership topics we discuss, knowing the concept exists and that some attention needs to be given to it is far more important than the specifics of how we do it.

It could start as simple as a spreadsheet that lists:

- Date of Assessment

- Data Source

- Data Attribute

- Intended Use

- Suitability Evaluation

- Assessor Name

Maybe it starts as a reference document published as part of your data services offerings. Down the road, you could add these findings into a tool that provides integrated insights so that data consumers have this information alongside the data itself.

Everything with Data Quality outlined above should seem obvious, yet very few organizations seems to have figured this out. If we agree that data needs to be suitable for its intended use, then without any guidance on what that suitability is, what will rational people do? They will assume the data is perfect, and when it turns out not to be perfect, they stop trusting the data. They will then blame the data people who provided the information, because who else are they going to blame? We are the ones who are supposed to make sure the data is right! And they were never told that the data was unsuitable for their use.

MAKE-AN-IMPACT! If we continue letting people make blind assumptions about data's suitability-for-use, we will never make Data Quality better in our organizations.

If nothing else, we must educate folks that imperfect data can be trusted. We also have to inform people when we know the data is unsuitable for the uses they intend. We can work with them to allocate resources and prioritization to hopefully help the data reach the usefulness they need, but without more transparency in our interactions, this problem will only get worse.

So now that we have an understanding of data's suitability-for-use, we probably can think of examples where the data in our companies currently isn't good enough to use for what people want. This gives us an opportunity to implement a Data Quality improvement initiative that has measurable objectives. We can say things like, "Our data is currently a 75 overall Data Quality score, but for the intended use we need 85, so we must devote resources to improve the completeness and verified sub-scores by 20 percent. This will require approximately 60 hours of effort at $X per hour."

At the same time, we can tie the intended use to a Data Value creation estimate, and then compare the costs to expected benefits to inform the prioritization of what we actually do! Using the Data Value principles we've discussed, we now have a quantification of our Data Quality improvement opportunities! We can do this kind of exercise for any of the DLF Disciplines, and then compare where we'll likely get our best return-on-investment (ROI).

But improving suboptimal Data Quality is only one option. If we are really concerned with maximizing ROI (or Data Value), we should evaluate the potential sources of Data Quality issues and take action to prevent those problems from creating data that will cause problems downstream. Cleaning up data is almost always a painful and costly exercise—best to avoid it entirely whenever possible. As in health, prevention is the best medicine!

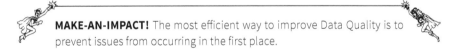

MAKE-AN-IMPACT! The most efficient way to improve Data Quality is to prevent issues from occurring in the first place.

We never have enough resources to do everything we would like to do. By quantifying value, we can optimally allocate scarce resources across any data initiatives we are considering, regardless whether they are Data Quality, Data Governance, systems-related, etc.

For true Data Quality aficionados, this quantified Data Quality approach should raise an eyebrow when extended to its logical limit. Though the common misconception (thoroughly debunked above, if I do say so myself), indicates a "perfection or nothing" default approach—the truth is that aiming for perfect Data Quality is always a mistake.

At the limit, diminishing marginal returns in the pursuit of perfection will consume infinite resources while driving zero meaningful difference in business outcomes. Executives often make decisions with 70 percent or less confidence-levels, as they cannot delay decisions until more complete information is available. Rocket scientists and pharmacists, by comparison, often require higher-levels of confidence before moving forward.

MAKE-AN-IMPACT! When there is a sufficiently high likelihood of the optimal result, stop trying to make the data better! There are other Data Quality problems that need solving.

Why keep trying to improve data that already drives the best possible business outcomes? Once the right decision or activity is likely, we must divert precious Data Quality improvement resources to data assets that need the help more.

But data rightfully now has people's attention, and we must start putting in better Data Quality practices that will help all of our organizations reach their potential. To correct the perception of Data Quality, we must have the courage to address these items head-on, and ensure that we make the most of any resources that come our way. With Data Quality scoring, suitability-for-use assessments, and issue prevention actions, we will truly help our organizations get better at what they do.

MAKE-AN-IMPACT! Being excellent at Data Quality provides an outstanding foundation for Data Leadership capabilities in every discipline.

Danette McGilvray, a valued peer reviewer of this book, has dedicated her career to helping organizations improve their Data Quality for the sake of their business needs. Her book *Executing Data Quality Projects: Ten Steps to Quality Data and Trusted Information*™ is highly-recommended for anybody serious about Data Leadership. Though starting with a Data Quality-centric perspective, the underlying principles are aligned with those found here.

Getting going with Data Quality is probably an important Data Refinement discipline for all organizations, and the next three Refinement disciplines build upon an assumption that Data Quality is sufficiently optimized. So as we compare to the other DLF Disciplines, Data Quality may not be the absolute highest priority on our list, but it should be close to the top.

 Master Data

Master Data Management, within which we are including Reference Data Management, is a discipline that collects and coordinates usage of the most frequently-used data sets in our organizations. Definitions of regions, product categories, customer classifications, states, and zip codes—these are but a few examples.

MAKE-AN-IMPACT! When Master Data is managed well, systems are easier to keep aligned, and data is able to flow more freely. When the same data is used in multiple places, but not managed holistically as one data set, these data sets will inevitably diverge over time.

People may have the best intentions, but without coordination even well-intended changes will cause differences. Then as the data is used throughout the respective systems, the uniqueness becomes more ingrained.

Reconciling incongruent Master Data sets is a special kind of painful. Think of a fast-growing company that has regional salespeople who earn commissions by what is sold in their areas. Over time, the company hires more people and modifies sales territories, but the system that tracks the actual sales is drawing its information from an outdated map. People manage their behavior based on how sales reports indicate they are doing. What happens if a technologist finds the error and fixes it without warning?

Chaos.

The salespeople think all their numbers are wrong. Executives are mad because things are not lining up to their expectations. Data Quality has arguably improved, but people are up in arms. Worse, since people have been operating on faulty information, they have inadvertently been generating commissions for other reps—and now management has lost the ability even to know which salespeople are the most productive.

This is the impact from one Master Data set that was updated somewhat slowly. Imagine the risk across most organizations that have no Master Data proficiency at all! How many data sets that should be the same actually have different versions?

Managing customer accounts as Master Data is a bit of a holy grail for Master Data programs. Some might argue that customer data can be too voluminous to truly be considered Master Data—my counterpoint is that if we mess up customer data, what do we plan to get right instead? Customer data is as important as it gets.

Customer data will need to be referenced by systems throughout the Data Lifecycle. Keeping it consistent is a high priority. Many organizations are challenged to define who their customers even are—let alone maintain data consistency throughout all of the systems that reference customers.

Where we should prioritize our organizations' Master Data efforts first may vary depending on our unique circumstances. As Data Quality and Metadata represent core functional competencies that can be applied in any data context, specific opportunities to take on Master Data challenges will become apparent over time. Thus, the Master Data DLF

Discipline represents a longer-term objective for organizations still trying to build the fundamentals.

MAKE-AN-IMPACT! From a strategic point-of-view, for organizations earlier on the data maturity curve, Master Data should be considered enough to avoid making things unnecessarily difficult for our future selves.

For example, if we are building out a new data mart, it would likely be a good use of energy to see if we can reuse existing customer sets—or even better, establish a lasting precedent for merging multiple customer sets into a consolidated customer master that can be extended throughout the organization. It may feel arduous or like scope-creep in the moment, but this kind of surgical strike with Master Data has the potential to save thousands of dollars (or more!) down the road.

 ## *Enrichment*

Data Quality helps us assess the data we have and, among other things, identify where the data is insufficient to meet our business needs. Sometimes we can fix things on our own, but other times we need to go outside our walls for added help.

MAKE-AN-IMPACT! Data Enrichment is supplementing our internally-available data sources with external resources. By definition, it is additive and will supply context to data that you already have (it's Metadata, just like pretty much everything!).

As with all things data, we need to be judicious in how we obtain external resources. Some will be provided for a cost, while other data sources will be free. Be wary of free data, especially if not coming from public/open data sources. Under the best circumstances, free data sources may not be easy to use, or infrequently updated, or formatted in an arcane method used about as often as Latin. In the worst circumstances, the data may be incomplete, inaccurate, or unauthorized—and by using it we may face serious legal consequences.

Enrichment resources available for a fee tend to follow the "you-get-what-you-pay-for" rule. Dun and Bradstreet, for example, has amassed a staggering amount of highly-curated information about businesses of all kinds. They know their information is prized, so they charge a premium for it. Deciding whether it is an attractive return-on-investment is going to be a different exercise for every organization.

One of my favorite free and public data sources for Data Enrichment is the National Oceanic and Atmospheric Administration (NOAA.gov) website. They provide a rich resource of weather information gathered from weather stations throughout the world. This information is great for establishing weather-based analysis to identify patterns in customer behavior, employee absenteeism, and other product performance metrics.

Every organization should be looking at weather information to help assess past performance and predict future behaviors. If we could do something as simple as avoid under- and over-staffing situations, what would the outcome be worth? A lot!

This is exciting one-step-removed-from-actual-value kind of data analysis—you bet that's the kind of impact we want to make! From there, we can build upon our rudimentary weather analysis and find supplementary data to build models that help us understand the influence of everything from holidays to conventions to what the impact is when the VFW hall next door hosts a fish fry.

And that last one is important! Not only do we super-love the idea of old-school fish fries, but we don't need to work for a large organization to make this worthwhile.

 MAKE-AN-IMPACT! Any individual reading this book has the mental fortitude to learn how to acquire data, put it into a place where they can work with it, and then do some analysis that will help their business.

Even if we are looking at daily cash deposit amounts from a bank statement against daily high temps in our area from NOAA, it may tell us a story that helps us do something different to make our business better. Will every Data Enrichment opportunity be hugely beneficial, or even worth the effort? Nope. Not even close. But it is still worth it, because those that work out will exceed the cost of effort from all of them.

Like I mentioned earlier, doing a lot of Data Enrichment is of minimal value before our Metadata and Data Quality capabilities are in good shape. But once core capabilities have been established, Data Enrichment can become a valuable addition to our Data Value story. As we go down the path of adding more to our data, we run the risk of creating so much that people lose sight of what is most worthwhile—or we inadvertently spend too much energy maintaining data sources and outputs that are not worth the effort.

 ## *Curation*

There is a lot going on in this DLF Category! Between Metadata, Data Quality, Master Data, and Enrichment, we have an impressive amount of potential value that we can create. With increasing potential value comes complexity, and complexity begets additional costs—and we do not like creating costs. This is why Curation is the final discipline within the Data Refinement category. We need to be deliberate about the data and capabilities in which we continue to invest, and those that are better off deprecated.

This is Data Curation: the art of removing what is not needed. This is not a standard definition of curation, but is intended to highlight what is important but often overlooked. When we think of curation, we tend to think of what is included, like in a museum gallery, because the exhibit is defined by what we see. But look around—everything is oriented toward what is included. Excellent curation is actually about removing anything unessential so that the important stuff shines through. Think of our objective as cultivating data bonsai trees.

 MAKE-AN-IMPACT! Just like we must focus our energy to create a balanced system of Data Leadership Categories, we can further boost efficiency by actively removing unnecessary waste from the system.

Though we might think this is all implied as part of other DLF Disciplines, in practice it is largely overlooked. People are wired to come up with new ideas and pursue them. We like to have brainstorming sessions where we think of anything and everything that might expand our capabilities. Anyone who has ever been in a brainstorming session knows that most of the ideas are embarrassingly terrible, but a few special ideas have enough potential to be worth taking further action. These justify the meeting because we see the opportunity to add value by taking action—this mentality aligning to the *increasing revenue* part of the Data Value equation.

Just as "a dollar saved is as good as a dollar earned," we should spend as much effort assessing the value of shutting down underperforming activities as we do brainstorming new ones. Why don't we ever have "anti-brainstorming" meetings where we actively abandon our current activities not living up to their potential?

These meetings would likely be more effective than brainstorming meetings, because we will have more data available to drive our conclusions! In any setting we are going to have a lot of valuable ideas, and even more that aren't worth it. It's the rough that comes along with the diamond. To get to the good stuff, we have to experiment—but we don't have to continue investing in the bad ideas once we know they are bad.

 MAKE-AN-IMPACT! The worst thing we can do is never make a mistake.

As we know by now, data is an imperfect art. We can have all of the data we want, refined and as suitable-for-use as it can be, analyzed with the best tools and techniques available, and we are still capable of making the wrong decision. This is because the future can't be predicted completely.

So this implies that if we wait to act until we are nearly-certain that we won't be wrong, we will have missed out on most of the possible value! Effecting business change, the source of Data Value, necessarily comes with some amount of risk. We normally think of this as a motivator to get moving, but what happens when we try to run in every direction at once? We get nowhere. We also probably look foolish flailing around like that.

Having the courage to lead means having the courage to be wrong. If we use those moments of wrong to learn and change our future behaviors, then next time we will be a little bit more likely to get it right. In poker, they say never chase bad money with good money—that means once we see we misjudged a situation and will lose the hand no matter what, we have to stop putting money into it. Fold our cards and find another opportunity.

Back in the data world, these same lessons apply. If we build data analysis tools that people don't use, we need to recalibrate the tools, provide more training, or get the right data into them. Data Curation is about observing the world around us, identifying the mistakes, and correcting our course of action. Throw that project plan away if it is not leading us down the right path.

Data Curation is too often overlooked by organizations focused on building new things. In fact, even most Data Management texts and frameworks make no mention of it. This makes balancing the scales a function of always adding more—and at some point the scales just cannot handle the weight. Whether that manifests in losing funding, or getting fired, or simply being relegated as unimportant, this will be our fate if we continue to ignore Data Curation.

MAKE-AN-IMPACT! This entire Data Refinement Category boils down to judiciously applying the resources we have to transform data to drive maximum business change.

The first two DLF Categories have focused more inwardly on what we can build and directly do with the data. The rest of the Data Leadership Framework focuses more outwardly on connecting the data to actually changing our businesses.

9 DLF ADOPTION: ACTING FROM DATA INSIGHTS

The third Data Leadership Framework Category is all about connecting people to the data we made useful during the first two DLF Categories. We may have built up considerable potential value in those activities, but that potential value will not become realized without people putting it to use.

People can use data in countless ways, and the DLF Disciplines that we outline in this Category are intended to be representative, but not necessarily comprehensive.

MAKE-AN-IMPACT! Since creating Data Value depends on organizational change, once we have data worth using, we should refocus most of our effort toward connecting data to the change catalysts in our companies.

Just like with Data Quality, this is simply saying that we should not keep focusing our energies on making data better if we are struggling to realize the value that is already there. The right way to do this is to get our businesses to leverage the basic insights first, like we talked about with the weather analysis in the Data Enrichment section. Then we can learn from how the data drives positive change, and we can use that knowledge to improve what we do with the data going forward. Hey! How did the Simple Virtuous Cycle sneak back in here? It's everywhere, that's why!

So as we get into the details of the Adoption Category, remember that these too are guides to help us think through our data-related challenges and opportunities from all directions. These are not prescriptive solutions on which to take a check-the-box mentality. It's probably clear by now that around these parts we aren't too fond of "check-the-box mentalities" under most circumstances. It is something we need to do from time to time, but it's very rarely the right way to arrive at the best solution.

Data Modeling and Warehousing

This one is close to my heart. Actually, this one is close to many people's hearts, because Data Models and Data Warehouses are often the beating hearts of organizational data capabilities. These are our classic, relational-database-backed cornerstones enterprise data environments—responsible for a large part of the Data Value created in today's organizations. Many of the reports, dashboards, and visualizations that we build couldn't be created or maintained as effectively without a Data Warehouse sitting underneath it. Before we get into the specifics, let's first make sure we understand the definitions:

Data Modeling is how we take our understanding of truth and put the data that describes it into a form that both accurately reflects and efficiently delivers the information to those who wish to use it. Data Modeling is how raw data gets structure—most commonly in databases, and for analytics purposes in Data Warehouses.

Data Warehouses were all the rage a decade or two ago—and for good reason. Data Warehouses are very good at a lot of things. If we want to serve up information to a variety of changing Data Consumption mechanisms for operational purposes, Data Warehouses have us covered. They provide consistency and performance to data consumers, but require substantial effort to build.

 MAKE-AN-IMPACT! Data Modeling and Data Warehousing are often grouped together because we cannot accomplish much Data Warehousing without models, and our Data Models don't accomplish much without being in a database.

For Data Analytics purposes, this is most commonly a Data Warehouse database. Though this symbiotic (or co-dependent) relationship is real, it should in no way diminish the depth and importance of either Data Modeling or Data Warehousing. People can have entire careers as Data Modelers, and some of the greatest thought leaders in the Data Management space are primarily Data Modelers at heart.

Similarly, Data Warehousing professionals often have deep, specialized skillsets that combine technical proficiency in relational databases with the ability to design and shepherd the data flows throughout them.

In a lot of ways, Data Modelers are the business side of the Data Architecture coin. Data Modelers create the conceptual and logical designs for data containment, and hand it off to the physical designs led by Data Warehousing folks.

MAKE-AN-IMPACT! We might think of Data Modeling as designing how actual truth (real-life) becomes approximated truth (data).

We have talked a little bit about Data Modeling and Warehousing, but we have not yet addressed one key question about this DLF Discipline. Are you thinking of it? The most obvious question is:

"What the heck is Data Modeling and Warehousing doing in the Adoption Category?"

This, at first, seems to be a good question. The specific functions performed in both Data Modeling and Data Warehousing are certainly similar to those that we find throughout the Data Access and Data Refinement Categories. We're obviously working with the data, building structures, and creating systems and platforms to do things.

The big shift in the Data Modeling and Warehousing Disciplines is that we're now focused on the consumption of the data. Data Warehouses used to be necessary for a range of data processing tasks, and ten or twenty years ago this may have pulled it into an earlier DLF Category. But now, because there are so many ways to transform and move data that are not part of the Data Warehouse, we no longer see data processing as an essential role of the Data Warehouse. The Data Modeling and Warehousing of today are mostly concerned with the way people need to consume the data. This is the definition of Data Adoption, so that's why we're here.

Though we argue that Data Modeling and Warehousing is part of Data Adoption, the most important thing is that we create maximum Data Value. If moving this Discipline to another DLF Category would help us create more Data Value, we would move it immediately. We can't stress enough that these DLF Categories and Disciplines are adaptable: rename them, move them around, and even combine Categories if necessary. Whatever it takes to make the biggest impact in our businesses. Let's just be thoughtful in the tradeoffs, and we'll be okay—especially if the concepts are staying in the same spot, but the titles are changing.

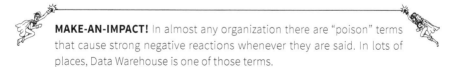

MAKE-AN-IMPACT! In almost any organization there are "poison" terms that cause strong negative reactions whenever they are said. In lots of places, Data Warehouse is one of those terms.

Seems like a rite of passage that organizations have one or two colossal Data Warehouse failures before they finally get it right. Data Governance is also way up there in the don't-say-that-around-here hall of fame.

Regardless of what we choose to call them, Data Modeling and Warehousing are not to be overlooked. Despite the fact that technology has become amazingly powerful, do not fall into the trap of thinking that these are functions we no longer need. An in-memory visualization tool, for example, is not an adequate replacement for a properly-modeled data layer. Even Artificial Intelligence is incapable (so far) of replacing a human's unique ability to model a database to fit an organization's specific data needs.

Just like Data Warehouses are no longer necessary to do the Access and Refinement functions, they are also only part of the equation for serving up data in efficient ways. Data used less frequently can be left in less-warm, file-based storage instead of in the Data Warehouse proper. Technology now allows us to directly query those files without needing to perform any other file movements—the future is now!

MAKE-AN-IMPACT! Think of these cutting-edge technologies as complements to the traditional Data Warehouse, not replacements for it.

With all of these improvements in technology, the right mix of capabilities for a firm is going to be different than that of any other. The complexity of Data Modeling and Warehousing actually increases as the variety of technology options grows! We certainly see some overlap between these and areas like Data Architecture and Enterprise Architecture.

This evolution is likely to continue at an ever-increasing rate. Though this domain of thought is not likely to go anywhere anytime soon, the longer it has been since this was originally published, the more the specifics will have continued to shift. If nothing else, working in the data space will keep us on our toes!

 ### *Traditional Reporting*

Data Warehouses do not do too much just sitting there by themselves. We need to get information out of them, and the simplest way to do that is through reports. Traditional Reporting is a one-directional flow of information out of a data repository into something that a person uses. This could be text/numeric or graphical outputs sent to paper (or PDF), or often put into a spreadsheet like Microsoft Excel.

From there a person will work with the information, either using it to directly influence their business activities and decisions (good job!), or doing additional manual data manipulation and analysis to reach the point where they can put the report to use (a possible opportunity for improvement!).

MAKE-AN-IMPACT! What separates Traditional Reporting from other information-sharing mechanisms is that once the report is created, information does not flow directly back into the data repository.

This is a limitation, certainly, but it is not necessarily a bad thing. Compared to other options, it is a lot easier and faster to write a query to pull information from a Data Warehouse and export it into a PDF or Excel file. We can always establish information feedback loops further downstream that will re-capture the data created from actions taken based on the reports.

Where things get dangerous is when we provide a report that is then manually integrated with a system outside our knowledge. It is perfectly reasonable to do this for exploratory and prototyping purposes, but many organizations fail to thoughtfully operationalize these early efforts. When that begins to happen frequently, do you know what that is called?

A big mess.

We apparently don't have an obtuse term for everything in Data Management! Having too many manual processes, Excel sprawl, or no clear knowledge of which reports are actually useful and which are worthless—these are real challenges faced by countless organizations. Many data analysts and data scientists spend considerably more time manipulating data instead of performing the analysis they were hired to do.

Reporting remains a fundamentally important capability today, and it will continue to have a role in organizations far into the future. Just like we must deliberately measure and improve balance across all DLF Disciplines, Reporting is part of this. When considering this, the first steps include: quantifying the level of effort to produce the reports themselves, then assessing the reports' usefulness, and then determining their contribution to actual Data Value through business impacts.

Some organizations do not bother with this kind of meta-analysis of reporting because "There's no time" and other such nonsense. This is the kind of misguided prioritization that causes things like Excel sprawl and the proliferation of useless reports in the first place. We must break this cycle of simply trying to run in every direction to keep up with the countless demands for our attention and energy!

MAKE-AN-IMPACT! Anyone who claims they do not have time to compile and measure performance data inevitably wastes a lot of time.

How could they not? Do they have a magical sense of intuition that allows them to know all of the relative value of their own behaviors? Can they even articulate what their value proposition, let alone value creation, actually is? How do they ever improve without evidence of areas in which to improve? Are they claiming to be perfect? Are they the first perfect person? Are we that lucky to actually work with the world's first perfect person? Holy cow, should we order a cake or something? Does anybody know the number to the cake place?

Just seeing if you were paying attention amid all of those questions, but the point is still valid. Once again, we can recall the Simple Virtuous Cycle: Measure, Identify Improvements, Improve.

MAKE-AN-IMPACT! Reporting can be drastically improved if we simply hold ourselves accountable to understand how people actually use the reports we create.

Even with relatively simple reporting, optimizing what is there will likely pay huge dividends. Granted, turning off a report does not typically save a ton of money straight away, but reducing the operational load, not to mention the support costs, adds up over time. Think of Traditional Reporting as low-hanging fruit. So how about we move up the tree a little?

Interactive Dashboards and Visualizations

Traditional Reporting is to Interactive Dashboards and Visualizations like photographs are to video games. Though a photograph tells a thousand words, a video game lets you battle Bowser. Which is more valuable? As any kid will tell us, video games are definitely the way to go. It's not even close. Similarly, wouldn't everybody rather have a report they can do stuff with, rather than just a static image to look at? You betcha!

Data Dashboards were amazing developments in the '90s and early 2000s. They were graphical and easy-to-consume depictions of useful information. Some fancy ones even let us do a bit of filtering. This was groundbreaking at the time, because we hadn't had much exposure to this kind of information delivery mechanism—at least not without significant manual effort or large technology investment. Plus, being a stockbroker seemed super-cool, and they were always shown looking at a bunch of screens with charts all over them.

Now we can do most of that stuff on a watch.

Today's Interactive Dashboards and Visualizations are next-level: drag-and-drop fields, report chart type selection on the fly, joining data sets at the application-level—not to mention advanced aggregation and custom-function creation. All of it in real-time!

And all of those we can now do on a phone.

If we want to be bold and actually use a computer, this is where we can simply load files into memory and do all the analysis that used to require Data Warehouses and sophisticated cubes. That said, lots of times it's still much simpler to use a Data Warehouse instead of files, driving more from the ease-of-administration versus a processing-power constraint.

MAKE-AN-IMPACT! Our laptops today are plenty capable of storing and processing more data than many companies have. Across many use cases, we live in a post-computing-horsepower-constrained world.

If we are no longer constrained by our technical limitations, where does the bottleneck shift? Look in the mirror! We, the people, are now the weakest link! We are fundamentally limited by our abilities to consume and react to the data served to us at a pace that far exceeds our input capacities. Don't be too sad about it, though, because there is a silver lining to this cloud of disappointment.

 MAKE-AN-IMPACT! Now that computing capacity universally exceeds our own, we get to compete on process design!

Sure, that may not seem all that exciting, especially since so many of our organizations seem so dreadfully bad at creating efficient processes. But it has to be better now that we do not need to wait six months for that new server rack to arrive. We can design, implement, redesign, and reimplement many times over! There's that Simple Virtuous Cycle sneaking in again. Since we've covered that already, let's dive deeper into the Visualization part of this DLF Discipline.

Visualization tools enable analysts and other information workers to curate stories that can be presented to the end data consumers. These are like slide shows of interactive charts that help highlight the most interesting findings, but also allow the end user to interact with them just as if they started with a blank screen in the interface. I've been involved with many presentations that use these tools, and very few data delivery mechanisms can reach the top of the org chart with comparable pop.

Because of their executive-level reach, Interactive Dashboards and Visualizations should be among the top priorities for nearly all organizations. They are quite simply too powerful to be left on the bench. Even SQL-fluent individuals like myself will accomplish more by leveraging the incredible power of Data Visualizations.

The new breed of ad hoc Data Wrangling and Visualization tools can bypass the bigger ETL and Data Warehouse dynamics, often temporarily or as a proof-of-concept. Using these tools, single individuals without programming backgrounds can execute an entire Data Value Chain without additional help! In some organizations, this is considered bad, with "Shadow IT" a common term that gets thrown around to describe non-approved technology use.

 MAKE-AN-IMPACT! Data Leaders love to find Shadow IT, as it is evidence of folks who are so committed to creating Data Value that they are willing to break the rules to do it. Their tactics may need some adjusting, but their hearts are in the right place!

Based on our understanding of Data Value, we should embrace these kinds of efforts, at least within reason. As long as the net outcome is positive, what do we have to fear? Or is this a setup? Perhaps a valid perspective of one side of the story whereas in the next section we will balance it with an equally-compelling perspective from the other side? That's feeling likely.

Systems Integration

This is another DLF Discipline that at first blush may seem to be in the wrong Category. Shouldn't Systems Integration go in the Access category? Well, no, because we would have put it there if that's where it should go.

The reason Systems Integration is in the Adoption Category is that it is an automated data consumption mechanism. Consider: if a person reads a reporting output, analyzes it, and then performs some sort of action driven by the new knowledge—the most efficient improvement would be to eliminate the manual efforts entirely. If we can string together the data sources, analysis, and resulting actions, then people can spend their time on more valuable pursuits. Or maybe just go get a coffee instead; we won't judge.

Determining the algorithms and specific business process automation falls in the Impact category, but Systems Integration represents the early stages where we need various independent systems to share basic information to ease data consumption and use.

Here is a real-world example: There is a city undertaking a multimillion dollar effort to replace all of the old-school streetlights in the city with more energy-efficient, smart LED lights. In addition to the energy savings, smart lights can be centrally controlled and actively monitored—so the system is aware of light outages before a citizen needs to call it in.

When city workers use the centralized smart lighting interface, they can obviously see information that pertains to the lights, since this information was generated by the lighting system itself. The folks building this system also thought it would be useful to have some information about electrical circuits, which are tracked separately in the transportation department's Graphical Information System (GIS) database. The GIS data was sent to the smart lighting application via a system integration.

Though it didn't directly automate a business outcome, it certainly saves time by allowing city personnel to access all of the pertinent information through one user interface. Now if a citizen calls about a streetlight being out, city personnel can immediately check to see if its entire circuit is down and scheduled for repair, or see that this light has not been previously reported by the system and may be malfunctioning.

MAKE-AN-IMPACT! Systems integration is an important consideration for us because the best way to create actionable information may not be through a separate tool, but to integrate data into something people are already using.

When our example GIS database was first created, nobody was thinking about the impact it might one day have in serving information to a futuristic smart lighting platform. The people building it only knew for sure that it might be called upon to serve needs they couldn't currently predict. Good thing for our example city that they built it that way!

Systems integration is typically not the highest priority consideration for us, but when it becomes important, it tends to become very important. It is also a function of seizing opportunities: if we are rolling out new systems, or making major changes, that can present us with avenues to work with information in innovative ways. We like that.

MAKE-AN-IMPACT! The best approach is to keep Systems Integration on the radar, and find those unique opportunities to plug into other initiatives to add a lot of value for minimal additional cost or effort.

As Data Leaders, we achieve our greatest impacts when people do not even think about the tools. We want them thinking about the insights they can draw from data—everything else is a distraction. The funny thing is that people really love distractions.

 ## *Emerging Data Technologies*

This DLF Discipline is all about the shiny objects that can easily distract our folks if we are not careful. Depending on our perspective, the good news or bad news is that emerging data technologies are a heckuva lot of fun for us Data Leaders, too! Who wouldn't want to play with the tech that is in the news and capturing everybody's imagination?

Emerging Technologies are like candy to Data Leaders. We want them, and they taste good when we get them. They may even give us a nice boost of energy for a little while! But then, once the sugar-rush wears off, we regret blowing our diet on them. It's not that Emerging Technologies are bad, it's just that they are not as nutritious to our organizations as more fundamental improvements to data capabilities.

We really should eat our vegetables before we have dessert. This is NOT the place to start—except when it is. This means that people are going to want fancy-pants Emerging Technologies, even when they do not have basic Reporting or core Access and Refinement capabilities. Just like most kids don't know why they should eat their spinach before indulging in the Kit-Kats, our data consumers don't know why they shouldn't have real-time streaming before they can balance the financial statements.

This presents us with somewhat of an ethical dilemma. As you now know from reading this far, we would probably be encouraging suboptimal resource investments if we let folks jump straight to Emerging Tech before getting the basics right. However, if we refuse to give them what they are asking for, they will simply replace us with someone else who will do it—and our replacement will likely not even know the path of pain they are heading down. That also seems suboptimal.

 MAKE-AN-IMPACT! The answer is a balanced solution that parents will find familiar: let them have a little candy as long as they eat their vegetables, too—we give them some cutting-edge tech to keep their interest, while also allocating enough resources to accomplish our core objectives.

This keeps the business sponsors interested, and gives us a chance of giving them something that will help in the end. This pattern happens more frequently than we would like. People have become conditioned to buy products and "quick fix" solutions rather than actually address the underlying problems. Data is too close to the nucleus of an organization to be solved by a single product, no matter how amazing it is (even if Apple made it).

 MAKE-AN-IMPACT! At this point we understand that data is our businesses, and we Data Leaders must be the masters of our own destiny, especially with Data Strategy, which is largely what this chapter has been about, while ostensibly discussing Emerging Technologies.

It's not all bad, as we can still buy ourselves a few toys along the way. How about we cheer ourselves up by looking at some of the particular Emerging Technologies we might consider?

As we've mentioned before, the goal is to introduce a few things worth researching further; these descriptions are short, subjective opinions that do not provide a particularly balanced view. Is that disclaimered-enough?

- **In-Memory:** This is as good a place as any to start. Tableau raised the bar for Interactive Dashboards and Visualizations, so much so that now that's what people often think about when they think of Business Intelligence tools. It's almost like Kleenex for data! Though the interactive and graphical capabilities are compelling, it's Tableau's ability to process data files and store them in-memory that allows users to do Interactive BI without an underlying database. It may be common now, but it is still very cool. Other tools have expanded on Tableau's power in the data processing space, and with today's computing power, put a staggering amount of Data Analytics power in the hands of a single analyst.

- **Graph Databases:** These are databases structured to understand the relationships between data. They facilitate smarter search capabilities where you do not have to guess the keyword precisely, which is bafflingly how many search tools still work. I'm looking at you, Microsoft! You too, Apple! Your desktop searches are an embarrassment, and both Siri and Cortana today are still effectively just voice-enabled versions of your long-standing text-based embarrassments. Amazon's Alexa is slightly better because at least she shops for stuff we don't need. In more successful use cases, graph database capabilities are transforming industries like document management and legal e-discovery. Think about it—with graphs on the back-end, coupled with Machine Learning and Artificial Intelligence (which get their own DLF Discipline for some good reasons you'll see later), human lawyers will be able to produce results at a much faster pace, which should eventually make legal services more cost-effective.

- **NoSQL:** This is hardly emerging technology, but there are plenty of companies (and data professionals!) that have not yet embraced the power of NoSQL, and this is both unsurprising and unacceptable. NoSQL is a technology that stores data in one of two forms: document or key-value pairs, the differences of which are less important right now than knowing those terms generally relate to NoSQL. This technology is particularly useful for quick retrieval of a specific data record that contains Metadata about the referenced item. Websites work this way, with IDs that get sent to the web server, which it then uses to query a NoSQL database to locate all of the information about our accounts. NoSQL does not do a very good job at aggregating information— if we are doing a lot of math, we're better off sticking with a relational database variant.

- **Graphical Information Systems (GIS):** GIS is completely taken for granted by us in our personal lives, but once learning how it works, it is mind-blowing. Our GPS systems rely on a precise understanding of latitude and longitude along with ultra-precise clocks. Oversimplified, a location is found by comparing the slight time differences received from a number of satellites and then a position is triangulated from those differences. The underlying database of addresses, roads, and terrain, composed of points and lines, is possible thanks to GIS. GPS systems are not the only use case for GIS—if we care about looking at anything through space and time, we care about GIS. When we think about what is on the horizon with Internet of Things (IoT), GIS is going to only get more important.

- **Cloud:** For anybody who has studied even basic economics, the benefits of the cloud should be fairly evident. The cloud involves sharing computing infrastructure investments across many organizations that do not drive their competitive advantage through unique hardware. For most organizations, if technology is a competitive differentiator, it is going to be through the software-layer. This implies that procuring commodity hardware with economies of scale is an optimal approach. Through the network effects of having many purchasers with differing consumption patterns, cloud technology providers like Amazon Web Services can create new computing consumption models never possible with on-premises infrastructure. We will talk more about the cloud later—but the power and economies are so compelling that any organization not moving in that direction is becoming an ostrich (i.e., head in the sand—unwilling to see the danger in their current situation).

- **Serverless:** Serverless runtime containers are at the logical limit of cloud infrastructure innovation. It used to be that we would have to manually instantiate a server instance to then run our code, but that either took significant ramp-up and ramp-down cycles, or we still had underutilized servers sitting around. Instead of provisioning a functional machine or VM (virtual machine), why bother with machine instantiation overhead at all? Cloud providers have now enabled runtime containers that allow us to execute code and simply pay for the computing power actually consumed. It simplifies developers' lives, and provides a near-perfect elasticity between utilization and costs.

- **Internet of Things (IoT):** The dream of the Twitter-enabled refrigerator is not what to think about with IoT. Instead, think about the smart watches that track your steps, sleep, and heart rate—and then allow you to visualize and track your health goals. Think about air quality sensors that enable text messaging if your allergy trigger is high today. Think about the manufacturing sensors that will give some of our oldest businesses incredible new insights on how to become more efficient. IoT is not going to have one killer app—it's going to be much more like a swarm of bees. One by itself won't change much, but a few billion will create a lot of honey—or sting a lot of people.

- **Python/R:** Python (and its Data-Sciencey cousin, R) merit mentioning because these programming languages have helped drive faster development processes, and play particularly nice in the cloud and IoT spaces. When I first learned Python, I was amazed. The syntax was straightforward and easy to write, but the biggest benefit came from how easy it is to extend. There is a centralized library where, with a single command, you can download already-written application capabilities to use in your code. This makes programming in Python more like assembling blocks, whereas other common languages require the developer to build up more from scratch. This may not be so impressive to folks who have been deep in the Linux world for a long time, but being unaware of this shared-building-blocks approach is often a blinder for those of us who have been isolated in the Windows or Oracle ecosystems for too long.

- **Blockchain:** Many folks are convinced that blockchain will be the next major technology disruptor.* A blockchain is effectively an immutable database that, in theory, cannot be corrupted due to its lack of centralized management. So think of Open Source, but instead of code, it's data—and instead of freely sharing the information with everybody, privacy is protected because everything in the blockchain is extra-encrypted with no way to reverse engineer without the source key. This secrecy-in-plain-sight approach enables cryptocurrencies, which have had a wild ride lately, but this is just the most well-known application of blockchain. The implications for health care, like electronic medical records that are perfectly up-to-date no matter which provider you visit, would potentially transform that industry. Every industry may have a similarly-compelling use case—but only time will tell.

While Emerging Data Technologies are exciting and get all our hope juices flowing, it is critically important to recognize that they represent only a small part of most organizations' Data Value Chain.

MAKE-AN-IMPACT! If we fail to excel at basic data capabilities, the advanced stuff will only amplify our problems.

At the same time, if we don't dream big, we are unlikely to get very far, either. The best approach is to treat Emerging Data Technologies like candy: it sure tastes good, but it is not enough to keep you healthy.

10   DLF IMPACT: MAXIMIZE BUSINESS OUTCOMES

It seems that many data-related initiatives are structured in the belief that if we create something that people use, that Data Value will be the inevitable outcome. This is wrong! Gaining Adoption is a necessary but insufficient step in creating Data Value. People can use data all day long but accomplish nothing meaningful in the end.

MAKE-AN-IMPACT! If we want to truly maximize Data Value, we must create a strong and deliberate connection between all DLF Categories and the business outcomes we hope to affect.

Data Leaders recognize that we can't leave value creation to chance, and that is what the entire DLF Impact Category is about. This category will not only help us tune our Data Value-generating efforts, but it will help us build credibility by quantifying the amount of value we create. This then feeds the business engagement activities that will amplify people's participation and the corresponding Data Value they create.

 Measurements, Metrics, KPIs

We cannot overstate the importance of measuring. Sustaining Data Value creation relies on measuring and responding to those measurements. When we talk about Measurements, Metrics, and KPIs, we are looking to use data to understand our business performance. This can be oriented to pure value by tracking revenues, costs, or risk management—but even more often it will be looking at the performance of Data Value's building blocks.

Before moving forward, let's clarify terminology. Do note that these definitions may vary somewhat across organizations, but should at least loosely align:

Measurements: Data, in the form of a number or state description, reflecting a truth about an object or process observation. Measurements can change over time, and can have correlations to business outcomes. They may or may not have relationships to anything that can be controlled, and may be internally or externally-created. Simple examples include temperature, quantity, length, weight, brightness, and cost.

Metrics: Measurements that are compiled with a comparative purpose in mind. Average temperature helps us know whether today's temperature is hotter or colder than normal. For a business, we want to identify Metrics that will give us meaningful insights to our business. If today's temperature is higher than normal, we may expect to sell more ice cream than we usually do, all other factors aside.

KPIs: Key Performance Indicators are special kind of Metrics that we exert influence over. Response rates, sales goals, customer satisfaction—these are high-powered artifacts that can show us whether we are doing well or badly relative to an established target. To create target values and ranges, we may employ scientific benchmarking against industry norms, or use the less-scientific approach of a manager's experience-driven whimsy.

Measurements, Metrics, and KPIs are the foundation of Data Value. We can build some fantastic capabilities upon these, but if we find ourselves in an organization getting serious about data but lacking these fundamentals, we know we have some serious work to do. The ability to build on these is why we advocate for everyone to first start measuring and understanding today's truths before trying to change everything.

MAKE-AN-IMPACT! All the technology in the world can't solve a paradoxical equation, which is exactly what we create when we want to measure progress with an undefined starting point.

We will never be successful if we cannot measure the impact we have made. These concepts should seem straightforward by now, though in practice the actual Measurements, Metrics, and KPIs can get out of hand quickly. We do not have to be rock-star data scientist unicorns to do this stuff. We just need to Measure, Identify Improvements, Improve, and repeat. We can pepper in the complexity over time, which will make things easier for people learning along with us, too.

It is not hard to find things to measure, especially if our business processes are creating data that is (or can be) stored in databases. The Measurements in those cases are already there, but we will want to push them further. We should identify which business activities are not currently throwing off or capturing data effectively, and how we might change that. It may require new sensors and IoT tech, or tweaks to business processes, but there is always a way.

Any half-decent manager should support better visibility into these things—but if we have to play some politics, it is often worth it. We should never forget that measuring processes, outputs, and efficiencies often sounds like oversight to folks, and can be interpreted as a threat. These fears are often overblown, but sometimes are perfectly justified. Especially in industries with longer histories, and less culture of data-driven evaluations, we should tread carefully when advocating for rapid change.

Once we establish Measurements, building toward Metrics and KPIs is more evolutionary. These will be pulled into existence by efforts in the other DLF Disciplines, and we can be a little more patient on those.

 MAKE-AN-IMPACT! The worst sin is to miss out on worthwhile Measurements by failing to capture and save data that will otherwise disappear forever. It is far more preferable having underutilized data versus losing data that we may someday need.

So we better prioritize this discipline accordingly, especially since we will not get very far in the rest of our DLF Impact efforts without a core competency in this area. For any imaginable data program, this DLF Discipline is likely a Top Five consideration. Once the triage stage is passed and we have baseline Measurements, Metrics, and KPIs, we can lower it on the list in favor of other value-building efforts, but this is one discipline that should always remain in our field of vision.

 ## *Regression Analysis and Predictive Modeling*

This discipline could more efficiently be labeled Statistics, but then nobody would read it. Isn't it hilarious that Data Science was coined as a sexy rebranding of Statistics, not unlike how people started eating Chilean sea bass only after they changed the name from Patagonian toothfish? Maybe *hilarious* is overstating it, but data jokes only get so good.

Out of principle, we're also fighting the instinct to call this section Data Science, since that term overlaps several of our DLF Disciplines. This whole branding of Data Science is fascinating. A layperson's definition seems to be: fancy stuff with numbers *and* programming that probably only people smarter than me can do. The only rational explanation for this is that people are irrationally afraid of numbers *and* programming.

 MAKE-AN-IMPACT! Data Science gains its superpowers from the vaguely-intimidating but equally tough-to-qualify responsibility set that varies considerably among different companies and teams.

Once we have Measurements, and perhaps even Metrics and KPIs, we will quickly move beyond the line chart ("Look—it goes up!") and into more sophisticated analyses. For those of us who once took a Statistics 101 course, this is a refresher of what we learned and immediately forgot about after the final. For those who haven't had the opportunity to forget a basic statistics curriculum, this is a very simple introduction that we'll move on from quickly:

Statistics relies on things called r-values and p-values, and the resulting correlation leads to an estimate and a +/- percentage level-of-confidence that our results are not mere coincidence. These are the humble beginnings of all the fancy Data Science that comes later.

Predictive Modeling takes Regressions and flips the direction—so that we can try to, ahem, predict the future through what happened in the past. Have we seen those disclaimers from financial companies? "The contents herein should be used for information purposes. Past performance does not guarantee future results." But isn't that exactly what they are trying to do?

Like all of the topics here, we are just scratching the surface—as statistics as a discipline is as old and deep as they come.

 MAKE-AN-IMPACT! A good strategy in the early days of a data program is to hitch our wagons with one or more numbers people who can dive into the details, but may struggle connecting their research to actions that improve business outcomes.

Since connecting data efforts to business outcomes is what Data Leaders do best, this is exactly the kind of partnering that Data Leaders should be looking to forge. We do not all need to be experts at doing the analysis, but if we can take the outputs and effect meaningful change, then everybody wins!

The priority we assign to this DLF Discipline will depend on a couple factors: First, can we do some of this analysis ourselves, or is there somebody in the organization with this skill set? It is a lot easier to source this internally than to hire from the outside or pay a high-priced consultant who does not know your business. Secondly, how ready is our data for this kind of analysis? If we have material Data Quality challenges, or our Measurements are inconsistently captured, then the more complicated Regression Analysis will not be as fruitful.

If our folks are already well into Data Adoption and clamoring for more depth of data insights, now we're talking! Remember not to take an if-we-build-it-they-will-come mentality here, and when to invest significantly in this area will come into focus at the right time.

 ### *Machine Learning and Artificial Intelligence*

Regression and Predictive Model Analysis is a bit dry compared to the new and exciting world of Machine Learning and Artificial Intelligence. These are two of today's hottest terms, and for good reason. These are how we can take enormous data sets and some generic notion of a pattern we'd like to investigate, and utilize the effectively unlimited computing power now available to us, and whittle it all down to actionable insights.

These two subjects are closely-related, but they are not exactly the same:

Artificial Intelligence: a branch of computer science attempting to build machines capable of intelligent behavior.

Machine Learning: Stanford University defines Machine Learning as "the science of getting computers to act without being explicitly programmed."*

Feels like Machine Learning is a little more approachable, right? This should be our mentality—let's use the machines to help us solve data challenges to improve our businesses, without necessarily trying to create sentient computer-beings.

Lest we think AI is about trying to create life, we should read the above definition a little closer. AI is about trying to make the machines behave intelligently. Many of us have the same challenge with our kids! We do not need computers to think like people, we just need them to clean up their rooms before bedtime without a big fight. That is, the benefit of AI systems is that they are generally rational, whereas children are highly irrational, especially when they are hungry or tired.

Based on our small, but strongly-correlated analogy, if we need something done without having to tell them a million times, give us less-theoretically-capable-but-way-more-rational Artificial Intelligence robots any time!

What is the problem with emotional, irrational children? They grow up to become emotional, irrational adults. These are the people on our teams, and even us!

This presents challenges for Data Leadership, regardless of what we do: even with the best outputs, the clearest conclusions, and highly-predictable business benefits, we have to hope that people will do the right thing in the end. Sadly, in reality, we cannot even be sure that people will act in their own best interests, let alone the company's.

There has been a lot of chatter lately about Artificial Intelligence taking over and destroying the world someday. That may or may not even be possible, but it is inherently frightening. Why is that? Wouldn't it be a better idea to entrust the future of the world to highly-intelligent, rational machines?

Of course not! That's crazy!

 MAKE-AN-IMPACT! Though people are emotional and irrational, and this can hurt our productivity from time to time, the complementary benefit is that we are also capable of empathy.

Sometimes we actually care about things that have no direct correlation to our own well-being. We will often act in opposition to our own self-interest because of a story that tugs on our heartstrings, or when giving our lunch to a homeless person will clearly help them more than us. Throughout history, people have willingly died for causes they believe in, and this could only be driven by irrational, emotional, empathetic, flawed, beautiful human beings.

And yes, we also do irrational things that are intentionally harmful to ourselves and others, too. Sadly, often without any rational reason at all—the pendulum is always swinging back and forth.

And this kind of unpredictability is a really tough thing to program.

Maybe none of this will impact our decisions to begin employing Machine Learning and Artificial Intelligence in our data programs—but with the pace of technology continuing to evolve ever more quickly, this may be a more valid concern than we think.

So where does this DLF Discipline fit into our balanced approach to Data Leadership? Normally, we would probably advocate saving this one for a little bit further into our journey. But if you recall the Emerging Data Technology section, there is a caveat: if your executives read something and are now excited to pursue an advanced Machine Learning and Artificial Intelligence strategy, we have one word: YES!

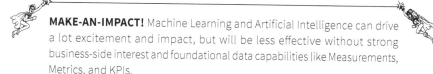

MAKE-AN-IMPACT! Machine Learning and Artificial Intelligence can drive a lot excitement and impact, but will be less effective without strong business-side interest and foundational data capabilities like Measurements, Metrics, and KPIs.

When we do have strong business-side interest, we must do whatever we can to nurture it. It's harder to build business interest in data than implement any specific data technology. When we are lucky enough to have people's attention, we had better not mess it up.

One factor changing the feasibility of Machine Learning and AI is that cloud platform providers like Amazon Web Services have rolled out services to make these tools much more accessible than they previously were. Entry-level costs are now approachable for pretty much any company looking to start working with these capabilities. This is both awesome and terrifying when we consider the number of people who now have access to potentially create "evil" Artificial Intelligence, or at least the number of people with companies with the Data Analytics potential to kick our butts in the competitive marketplace.

The above technically connotes the literal meaning of awesome, which often has a component of fear. But most of the time people think "awesome" is just another word for "great"—so we felt clarification was needed. We also feel that sometimes these anecdotes are a way to avoid writing more substantive content. How is that procrastination helping us? It's not. And then this becomes yet another example of silly, irrational, human behavior. See what we did there?

Business Process Automation

Business Process Automation is taking this rich tapestry of data capabilities we've covered throughout the DLF and applying them to directly drive business impacts! Remember all that stuff in the last section about irrational people not doing what the data tells them to do? That can all be history if we can just automate the processes entirely!

MAKE-AN-IMPACT! Business Process Automation can do amazing things when coupled to Machine Learning and Artificial Intelligence.

This is the dream: When we provide data capabilities to people, we help make their business decisions and activities ever more efficient. We Measure, Identify Improvements, and Improve until some of the decisions and activities can be automated entirely. That frees up the person to take on new decisions and activities that are less predictable.

Many of these Business Process Automation efforts are comparatively not that complicated, and the actual decision-making processes and resulting activities are often strikingly simple. Many information workers actually spend a startling amount of their time doing relatively low-value work that can be automated significantly, if not completely.

MAKE-AN-IMPACT! Look for Business Process Automation opportunities where people have already built their own data solutions and automations, often haphazardly, and with tools that are easy to use but difficult to scale or maintain.

For example, Microsoft Access is never the right answer for a production-level solution. It can do a lot of things quickly, and the skillset necessary to use it is not as technical as comparable tools. It's a fantastic option for creating proofs of concept or a temporary database to organize a potluck. Unfortunately, what makes it so user-friendly also makes it dangerous for many of the use cases where we see it incorrectly applied. The design decisions made in the software lead to an unwieldy, risk-laden tool that is prone to corruption and data loss.

A simple approach is to find anybody using Microsoft Access and then figure out how to replace it with a proper enterprise-grade tool. Sounds a little harsh, right? Using Microsoft Access for a production workload is like a hospital replacing all of its doctors with touchscreens and a popular self-diagnosing website. Microsoft Access is simply not the right tool for the task at hand.

This is not to say that people using Microsoft Access have bad intentions—they are just unaware that the software fills no enterprise functionality purpose in an organization. It simply fills a gap in knowledge of the appropriate tools. With data professionals on the case, we can bring Microsoft Access artifacts into a true database environment, along with the governance and data protections that will inevitably be necessary for something people cared enough to go out and build on their own. We can use SQL Server if we like Microsoft, or use something like PostgreSQL or Maria DB if we prefer free.

Another fruit-on-the-ground example is Excel Hell. People love to use Microsoft Excel for analysis because it is so flexible. It seems that Excel has a sizable lead as the most heavily used data analysis tool anywhere, probably by a factor of three. People love Excel, and rightfully so—it is an absolute gift to do basic iterative analysis and arrive at data-driven conclusions. The problem occurs when people start using it for repetitive tasks.

Once an Excel file is created, edited, and eventually shared, there should be a rule that the file is locked permanently and can never be edited again. If we want to make a new version, it must be created as a separate file. This would help keep us from losing data, which inevitably happens with Excel in the wild. It would not help us keep from making a huge mess, which also inevitably happens whenever Excel is freely used.

Once Excel is used to create something that will need to be reproduced, it should be adapted into a more formal mechanism, driven by consistent data sources. Interactive BI tools are great at this—we should use them!

In case this section feels like Microsoft-bashing, understand that the criticisms are not that Microsoft is making bad tools—it's actually the opposite! Microsoft's tools are so capable, and accessible to folks, that people can use them to accomplish a great deal. The downside is that people can build so much, so quickly, that their creations grow to a point where they become too difficult to maintain—and the resulting costs and/or risks degrade the investment returns of these efforts to the point where they consume more resources than they create benefits.

MAKE-AN-IMPACT! People want to use data to improve business decisions and activities, but they can't do it all themselves. Data Leaders must provide the right tools—but the goal is to automate business processes entirely when possible!

Sure, some business processes will never be fully automated. But we see so many business processes out there that are just people going through the motions because there is no other way available to them. This is a boring, sad existence for any person brilliant enough to work in our organizations. Let's help give them something more interesting to do—and then everybody wins!

Data Monetization

We have already talked exhaustively about Data Value, and we have discussed so many disciplines that work together to create Data Value. We get that most of this is complicated stuff, both conceptually and in what it takes to actually realize value through the coordination of everything. Well, compared to most, this one is pretty simple.

MAKE-AN-IMPACT! Data Monetization is about turning data into money by emphasizing the increasing revenue piece of the Data Value equation.

The most obvious way to do this is to sell data to others who find it valuable. This could take the form of selling email addresses to other companies that want to do marketing to our customers. Or it could be that upstream vendors want to better understand their market, so our data could inform them on how we ultimately serve the end consumers, and the vendor could respond by making more customized products.

People tend to not like being commoditized, so the example of selling raw data can particularly raise privacy concerns. Whenever monetizing data, we must be careful not to do something that could anger our customer base. The financial impact from that will likely far outweigh anything we would make through Data Monetization efforts.

Let us think about the second example for a moment—providing data to vendors for analysis. Assuming these insights are useful to the vendor, would it be more or less valuable to them if we could skip them the trouble of doing the analysis—and deliver it to them directly? This would save them effort and get at what they care about most, all while protecting the details of our customers' information.

Not unlike Data Quality, Data Monetization opportunities exist on a curve that shows the level of effort and resulting value alongside how removed we are from the atomic data. "Atomic data" is a common data warehousing term that means the data cannot be further reduced. For example, an order is made up of one-to-many items and related quantities. An order is not typically an atomic data point, but the order line items are.

The power of Data Monetization lies not purely in the data, but in the analytics that drive business outcomes. It is one thing to have data—all organizations do. But how many are making the most of the data they already have? Is the hypothesis that more data will help them really the most reasonable conclusion? What everyone needs are answers, not just data. Any Data Monetization effort should be acutely aware of this.

MAKE-AN-IMPACT! Data Monetization effectiveness can be a proxy for overall Data Value Chain effectiveness. No more pure measure exists for how much value is created than dollars directly generated from the corresponding activities.

This alone may tend to understate the truth, however, since directed efforts also tend to residually impact other areas. This will be even more true the further up the abstraction curve we go—advanced analysis is likely to have more wide-ranging implications than raw data alone.

The entire Impact category represents the capstone of the Data Value Chain, which we as Data Leaders are charged with maximizing. This is where we can review progress and identify improvements for the next iteration—completing the feedback loop and connecting us back to the beginning. In most of the areas we have covered so far we will always welcome help; they largely orient to things we can accomplish more directly.

11 DLF ALIGNMENT: ENGAGE STAKEHOLDERS

The final DLF Category is Align, which is less about the cyclical process covered by the other four categories and more about an ongoing set of services to help our organizations embrace the data capabilities we are building.

Field of Dreams (the movie) apparently continues to ruin the minds of data and technology professionals, decades after its release. In this classic '80s movie, a ghostly voice keeps saying, "If you build it, they will come," in reference to building a baseball field in the middle of an Iowa corn farm. And yes, the '80s were weird.

 MAKE-AN-IMPACT! This concept, "If we build it, they will come," unequivocally does not apply to data and analytics.

There are countless reports, interactive dashboards, and even entire Data Warehouses that are going completely unused or significantly underutilized. Some of these may have flawed designs, while others were built exceedingly well.

Ignoring those that missed the mark completely, what went wrong? Why wouldn't people fully embrace the data and analytics capabilities given to them? Don't they realize the power at their fingertips?

Of course they do not know the power at their fingertips! People are busy working! They are not sitting around waiting for us to save them. Simply building things and making them available is far from the full answer. We are going to need to explain, reach out, convince, teach, market, package, adjust, justify, prove, and ultimately sell our solutions to people to make the changes to achieve Data Value.

 MAKE-AN-IMPACT! It's up to Data Leaders to introduce people to data-related capabilities and ensure they have all the tools they need to be successful. We must realize and accept that nobody owes us a sale.

Strategy, Standards, and Policies

Sometimes we have to take our medicine. Standards and Policies are the elixir that will help our organizations put data assets to use at scale. This is where Data Governance sits, as well as Compliance and Regulatory mandates, and a host of other things that we have to do that we may or may not want to do.

These are also covered in excruciating detail by countless other Data Governance-related books. We will not go down that rabbit hole here, but rest assured that without reading at least a couple of these books, we will have a significant gap in this domain of knowledge.

Rather than rehash what so many other resources cover at length, what we will spend a little more time on here is the strategic aspect of this Discipline. Data Strategy is a big enough topic by itself. Let's begin by addressing the most important part first:

There is no such thing as a stand-alone Data Strategy. Data Value only comes through business impact—and business impact starts with Business Strategy.

MAKE-AN-IMPACT! Data Strategy is a highly-aligned, tactical manifestation of Business Strategy, and cannot be created nor exist independently if Data Value is the desired outcome.

Business Strategy is often what the executives come up with during a special retreat, often at a place that sounds made-up. One rarely hears of the transformative Executive Business Strategy retreat that happened in Cleveland.

Regardless, the Business Strategy is what ostensibly guides the decisions, activities, and ultimately the performance of our organizations. A Data Strategy outlines how our Data Leadership efforts align with the Business Strategy. A Data Strategy will cover more specifics on the DLF Disciplines that we intend to devote our energies toward, and even outline a roadmap of projects and milestones that we intend to undertake and reach, respectively.

A Data Strategy that is not fundamentally driven by Business Strategy may undertake worthwhile pursuits—but their relevance to business outcomes will be relegated to chance. This is wasteful, no doubt. But what if our business does not have a formal Business Strategy?

This is the case more often than we would hope. That said, nothing changes, except now instead of coming up with a Data Strategy, we first need to come up with what we think the Business Strategy is, even if nobody has written it down yet. Perhaps our executives are more operationally-focused, and are not actively developing larger-scale change initiatives that data might drive. If they need some help defining what the strategy might be, then we will have to be the ones to do it.

As Data Leaders, we cannot let any barrier stand in our way. Even if it means taking responsibility for articulating our companies' overall business goals. We will not decide the strategy for the executives, but we WILL document it.

MAKE-AN-IMPACT! If we take a cut at documenting the actual Business Strategy, and it turns out to be wildly incorrect, we can count on our executives letting us know.

Hmm. This whole notion of documenting the truth around us and then soliciting feedback and validation sounds awfully familiar. What could that be?

Right! This is a Metadata Management effort in disguise! Capture what the Business Strategy is and then we can have a meaningful conversation about what our Data Strategy *should be*.

To develop an excellent Data Strategy, we will also need to have a good grasp of our current capabilities from throughout the Data Leadership Framework. Once we have a baseline understanding of where we are, then we can begin to set a strategy to make changes. This is just like what we do in the Refine category, but instead of operating at the data-level, we are at the overall process level.

It isn't enough to simply execute the process and expect optimal outcomes. Effort improving the process will lead to greater improvements, every time. This hints at the philosophical core of Agile and DevOps. Rather than attempt to paraphrase the lessons, I recommend *The Phoenix Project* as an excellent resource to understand how information process design plays a pivotal role in everything we do with data. The book is actually about software development, but it really applies to anyone trying to catalyze transformative changes in an organization.

Once we understand our Business Strategy and can anchor it to our current data capabilities, we are in good shape. We will be able to craft a Data Strategy that is achievable and has measurable outcomes that will deliver real business impact. This is powerful stuff!

A well-designed Data Strategy accomplishes two things. First, it presents a clear vision of the future we're working toward—it answers why we are doing this. This is essential to helping motivate the folks whose efforts we will seek to make it happen. Second, our Data Strategy must answer how we will achieve this future-state vision.

MAKE-AN-IMPACT! Our Data Strategy must provide enough clarity into specific actions to give people hope that we will be able to transform strategic-vision into reality-vision.

Project and Program Management

On the heels of a rock-solid Data Strategy, our focus shifts to getting the real work moving. A Data Strategy by itself accomplishes nothing. We need a detailed coordination plan to help these five DLF Categories and 25 DLF Disciplines move forward in harmony.

A classical orchestra is an apt analogy here. The categories represent a class of instruments, like strings or percussion. The individual disciplines are a specific instrument type, like violins or xylophones. The overall amount of effort we put into specific disciplines are the number of players of that particular instrument. And Project and Program Management is the sheet music coordinating everyone's playing.

And guess who the conductor is?

 MAKE-AN-IMPACT! Data Leaders do the work ourselves when nobody else will, and we take full responsibility for the success or failure of every data-related endeavor in our organizations—whether we have control of it or not.

Though there may be countless reasons why we do not achieve our data goals, we never have a valid excuse. Our role as Data Leaders is to make maximum Data Value happen. Full stop.

Many of us may find that we do not even have good access into the existing Project and Program Management capabilities in our organizations. Project Management Offices are often their own domain, far removed from data concepts, and often held arms-length away from our IT friends. We may need to find a way into their club, or maybe in a worst-case-scenario we can operate independently as a data-focused "shadow-PMO."

That is not really an actual thing, but somehow we need to coordinate the many activities involved with creating Data Value. Let us assume that we have an ability to engage with the PMO. The first job is to figure out where their acute data challenges are, and find a way to help. Chances are there are ways in which our interests align with their needs, and we might be able to leverage their coordination mechanisms to facilitate our data activities.

The head of our organization's PMO is among the most important people a Data Leader can befriend, though it is debatable whether this person or the Chief Information Security Officer is the number one ally. We need to get things done, and even super-inefficient PMOs with terrible leadership are going to get us further than trying the terrible "shadow-PMO" idea we discussed briefly above.

MAKE-AN-IMPACT! While we have to break down barriers to ultimately transform our organizations, we should not get too crazy doing it. If we become labeled as a wild card it can be difficult to remain effective.

Managing organizational change is an entire career path by itself, and our PMO experts are usually better at it than we Data Leaders are. Our goal should be to influence their priorities so that they are taking into account the power of data to help the organization. After all, the mission of Project and Program Management resolves to the same thing as Data Value: influencing the revenues, costs, and risk management of an organization.

Marketing and Communications

We have touched on this in other sections, but just because we do something theoretically productive does not guarantee its actual positive impact on our organization. We have to sell it—help people understand why their lives will be better off if they use what we've built.

IT organizations have typically done this poorly. They build *whatever* at the direction of *whomever*, and then once it is delivered they generally leave it up to the business to make the most of it. The IT folks figure they will learn the rest of what they need to do via feature requests or bug reports. This is predicated on the flawed assumption that the business will communicate those needs back to them instead of complaining to each other that IT gave them another garbage solution.

It is through establishing real partnerships, while still embracing a level of personal responsibility, that ultimately leads to the Data Value that we are looking to create. Data Leaders cannot possibly succeed by chucking responsibility over the fence to the business— we ARE the business!

We also often find we do not have as much organizational control as we would like, so we have to catch some flies with honey! This means we have to use the powers of gentle persuasion to convince folks to help, or use what we've built, or buy some new tech, or pay our salaries.

MAKE-AN-IMPACT! Frustration is not a wholly-bad sign. Angry people are ready for change. They are in the fight, and they have not given up. If we can turn their anger and frustration toward hope and action, we can do anything!

Indifference, on the other hand, is a much tougher problem. Disengaged people simply do not care, so it becomes much more difficult to get them to take action. We have to somehow incentivize them to do more with data, but when they do not care about the shared benefits to the company, all we have is each individual's self-interest. That gets expensive.

It's arguably wise to align our Marketing and Communications efforts to feeding the self-interests of people who will do things to further our data goals. The problem is that people aren't actually all that great at doing things that optimize their overall self-interest. Appealing to people, as we discussed early on, is not a simple endeavor.

If we do not know what the optimal strategy to engage people is, we should focus on being the more appealing option compared to their next best alternatives. It helps if we are doing good things for them, too, but we know that alone isn't the best motivator.

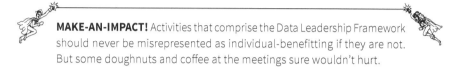

MAKE-AN-IMPACT! Activities that comprise the Data Leadership Framework should never be misrepresented as individual-benefitting if they are not. But some doughnuts and coffee at the meetings sure wouldn't hurt.

Incentives are the magic ingredient. A contest to see which department can drive the most revenue growth from Data Analytics may be a viable idea. Sharing cost reductions with employees is another common one. Even something as simple as public recognition or a bottle of wine can work wonders with things like Metadata business glossary definitions gathering.

The key is to give people something above and beyond when we ask them to go above and beyond. How that should manifest in any particular organization is a non-trivial exercise, and the answers will vary.

MAKE-AN-IMPACT! Most failed data programs did not deliberately design and coordinate their Marketing and Communications efforts. We cannot suffer that fate.

Organizational Training and Building Quantitative Culture

People are not going to understand what data can do unless we show them, and then teach them what they need to know to repeat it themselves. If we can give them the opportunity to work with data and have the experience be positive and productive, then they will become more motivated to build upon their initial skills and produce even better results.

MAKE-AN-IMPACT! An important goal is to build self-reinforcing systems that create their own momentum over time.

The first step in this is to introduce capabilities to people, even perhaps before the capabilities themselves are fully built. Wouldn't it be nice to get some insight into what people like, and where the opportunities for improvement are—before some grand unveiling that may unexpectedly miss the mark?

People will resist at the beginning. This is going to be true in any circumstance where the dreaded term change enters the picture. It is rarely worth going to excess trouble for a single possible benefit like training—but if we have secondary or tertiary benefits to be gained, like platform improvements, then it makes an outsized effort more compelling.

One organization I worked with that did a good job with Training and Culture is a large school district that employs about 45,000 people. They had an IT organization a fraction of the size they reasonably should have had, but the leadership was a strong proponent of Data Analytics. They created a data working group that spanned across the entire organization, and attracted over 40 self-selecting participants to regular workshops.

The working group leaders had created training materials and online walkthroughs, and the results were impressive. The data working group participants quickly made inroads using Data Analytics in their everyday work, and then they were able to spread the skills to others who were not formal data working group members.

This kind of train-the-trainer approach is essential to get widespread adoption. The organization in the above example had plenty of issues with data in other areas, but in this one area they uniquely excelled. The folks in the workshops were excited be learning SQL (SQL!) and were regularly taking what they were learning in the morning and applying it in their daily work by the afternoon. It was beautiful.

Now, we should all aspire to have that kind of training success, but it probably won't come easily. In fact, that same client had struggled for nearly a year to drive attendance and get the right format and participants, but they stuck with it. Something to be said for perseverance, certainly.

 MAKE-AN-IMPACT! In our pursuit of creating Data Value, taking action is more important than anything else.

Get out of the meeting room, find an opportunity to change things for the better, get the data dancing, and go MAKE-AN-IMPACT! Let's find a way to get away from talking about working and start actually working! Meetings alone will never change how we work, and if we don't change how we work, we will create no Data Value. If we lead by example, and create momentum through our actions, we can create a more quantitative culture inside our businesses.

Regulatory Compliance

This is fittingly the last discipline we cover in the Data Leadership Framework, because for so many organizations it is the triggering event behind doing Data Governance and other Data Management activities. Though we generally advocate an innovation-centric approach to data-driven change, being told by an auditor, or a regulator, or any external entity that we must comply with something is often the main initial motivator for organizations. We can loosely group audit findings, certifications, and any other arbitrary rules we decide to follow in this "Regulatory Compliance" section.

MAKE-AN-IMPACT! Focusing on Regulatory Compliance alone rarely leads to lasting Data Leadership.

An overemphasis on Regulatory Compliance is like when people memorize the answers for a certification test, pass it, and then subsequently fail because they aren't actually any good at what the certification said they could do. When we use this kind of thinking to spearhead Data Leadership, we will fall into the same trap but at an organization-level. We may succeed in checking the auditor's box but we will miss out on creating Data Value.

Remember how we've often said that Data Value is the only thing that matters? Regulatory Compliance is a way to potentially create Data Value—but it is not the same thing as creating real Data Value. Complying with regulations allows us to mitigate risk, and potentially increase revenues or decrease costs. Those are good things, and we should by all means add them to the list of ways we create Data Value. But there is so much more potential here than simply passing a test.

MAKE-AN-IMPACT! If our organizations are asking for it, we should devote some energies to Regulatory Compliance—because as much as we wish it weren't the triggering factor, it is where organizations often start their Data Leadership journey.

We're going to try to expand everyone's horizons to see the true potential of data-driven change, but we also need to work with what we've got. And this is certainly better than starting with no support.

So what do we do?

First, we need to know the specific sets of rules with which we need to comply. Determining this may be a function of our compliance department—or it could fall to lawyers, risk management, or our finance and accounting folks. It will vary from organization to organization. Once we start digging into all of this, it is certain to unveil a whole universe of headaches that we may, quite frankly, wish we never had to worry about.

A common example is the General Data Protection Regulation (GDPR), which is a European Union creation that provides strict rules on how organizations can use and must protect information for any EU-covered person. While many Americans may think, *Who cares, that's not our problem*—the fact is that any company that does business with an EU person must comply, even if it is on U.S. soil. So if a person from the EU comes to visit our hotel, or rents equipment from us, or has us paint their house—we may need to worry about GDPR.

Sure, we might question how the EU would be able to enforce these restrictions on a local company. They probably can't. But if we represent a larger business with global operations and deeper pockets, the EU may be much more likely to track us down.

 MAKE-AN-IMPACT! When to fully comply and when to take our chances is outside the scope of this book, but from a Data Leadership point-of-view we must find a way to align our organization's data efforts with the strategic decisions made as a business.

This is one example of a regulation that we could easily miss, but may find that we unwittingly violated. Should we have an unexpected and unintended data breach (aren't they all?), we may find that we are in violation of many regulatory constraints that we didn't even know about. Herein lies the fallacy that a check-the-box approach will ever be sufficient—they will always be adding boxes for us to check.

 MAKE-AN-IMPACT! With true Data Leadership we will be building the right organizational competencies to address the ever-increasing volume and variety of regulatory mandates, often satisfying them prior to their existence.

Data is becoming recognized as one of the most important assets an organization has, and our responsibilities as custodians of that data are increasing in kind. We must help our organizations manage the power and the risks of data due to market forces and the rules that we are required to follow. Data Leaders should evolve beyond reacting to requests to taking a more proactive role in how our organizations address Regulatory Compliance.

Closing Thoughts on the Data Leadership Framework

We have now covered the DLF at its highest level, and it feels like we are finally ready to get started. The depth of each of the 25 DLF Disciplines cannot be understated. Most could (and do!) have their own dedicated books focused on the specific subjects. In the context of Data Leadership, we have established a rudimentary understanding of what each of these is, but mastering them will take a lifetime. Just like Othello.

Even career Data Management folks are not experts in everything. The strongest Data Leaders will typically have deep backgrounds in one to three of the DLF Disciplines, meaningful experience in a dozen, and hopefully a hearty appreciation for the rest.

MAKE-AN-IMPACT! By establishing a team around us that can compensate for our own weaknesses, we will be able to bring a complete vision to our companies alongside the abilities to back it up.

The Data Leadership Framework is not a prescriptive tool that will tell us exactly what to do. In fact, on a first read it probably has us asking more questions than it answers. On subsequent reads it will do the same thing—and this is exactly the intent. The path to Data Value is winding, and nobody can predict exactly what is around the next turn. All we can do is prepare for the challenges we might face.

Balance is key to maximizing the throughput of our Data Value Chain. First we must evaluate the balance across the five DLF Categories, which should always be in relative lockstep with their overall capabilities. To keep the Categories in balance, we will deliberately choose which among the 25 DLF Disciplines to put energies toward to achieve the most impact with the minimum amount of cost.

MAKE-AN-IMPACT! Data Leadership is not rocket science—controlled explosions are more predictable than people.

In many ways, Data Leadership is among the most challenging professions an information worker can choose. But when done well, Data Leadership will completely transform our companies for the better. This path makes for a wonderful career, though I'm admittedly biased.

PART 3: DATA LEADERSHIP IN ACTION

12 BUILDING DATA LEADERSHIP TEAMS

The Data Leadership Framework is, at its best, a useful but incomplete reference architecture to help us navigate our Data Leadership journeys. We must fill in the details with our unique circumstances—and the priorities are going to vary for every organization, too.

MAKE-AN-IMPACT! The DLF strives not to provide the answers, but to provide a structured approach in organizing our many questions.

Businesses run in countless different ways. Executive leaders have usually spent multiple decades building experience and learning how to be successful in various roles, and they are going to primarily trust what got them to this point. They have built reliable instincts that have served them well.

Data Analytics has likely long been part of what these folks do. They have been receiving reports and taking action on the insights contained inside them for a long time. Occasionally they will ask for something new or a different kind of detailed breakdown, but most requests are built on top of what they already have, and largely rooted in their trusty instincts. At lower levels of an organization, the pattern is similar, but the data has a finer granularity and the resulting actions are more departmental and operations-oriented.

MAKE-AN-IMPACT! People at all levels of an organization find that their intuitions are often reinforced by data, and vice-versa.

The point is that data has surrounded us for a long time, and that it has been used for just as long. What is different today is that our ability to realize value from data is inching forward while the potential value of data is increasing exponentially. By failing to realize a significant percentage of data's potential value we incur tremendous opportunity costs.

"We have so much to do." "Data challenges are complex." "Coordinating people is hard." "Everybody has a day job." "We are all looking out for number one." "Submit a ticket for that request." "That needs approval." "We can't give you that." "I didn't have time." "Let's have a meeting to discuss." "Sorry, I had a conflict."

Countless reasons (or excuses) exist to slow down or stop. Our corporate default seems to be to delay for anything. What if we could make the standard "go faster unless otherwise proven necessary?"

MAKE-AN-IMPACT! We have an intuitive sense that momentum is good, but our own workplace norms betray that.

Look at sports, where the rules and options for success are more limited than in business, resulting in outcomes where winners and losers are clearly identified. How often does the winning team move slower or less decisively than the loser? Reckless decisions are severely punished or rewarded, but a recipe for disaster in any sport is playing "not to lose." Why would our companies, or our data efforts, be any different?

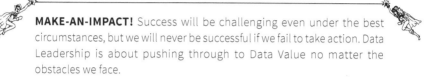

MAKE-AN-IMPACT! Success will be challenging even under the best circumstances, but we will never be successful if we fail to take action. Data Leadership is about pushing through to Data Value no matter the obstacles we face.

I once did some consulting work for an insurance broker. This is the kind of company that does not directly carry risk, but instead helps connect people who need insurance with the people who provide insurance. They had many lines of business that grew from that, but they all had a similar pattern of providing B-to-B services related to insurance.

Like many financial services organizations, numbers were everywhere. They were swimming in data, and they had significant challenges trying to manage it all, which I and my colleagues were helping them do. But this is not the point of the story.

The most striking memory I have of that client is that despite its business being fundamentally ruled by analytics, with seriously sophisticated underwriting and risk management capabilities, as we moved higher in the organization the numbers seemed to become less important. It was as if higher level decision-making justified a lack of Data Analytics rigor.

They managed this large company by the proverbial "gut instinct."

Of course they received plenty of reports, which they did not trust. They paid lip service to the idea of Data Governance, but the one executive who spearheaded the whole effort could not muster the broad support necessary to get widespread adoption. At the end of the day, the executives were "old school" insurance brokers, focused on their relationships and how things felt instead of what the data was telling them. Though this company has continued to perform fine, they will never know where they could be right now if they had maximized their Data Value.

MAKE-AN-IMPACT! There is no good reason to ignore Data Analytics that already exist—if you are already on a good path, it can only help.

What business leaders need is a better ability to integrate Data Analytics with their "proven" intuition. Ideally, for the leader, their intuition-based decisions will demonstrate their brilliance—and even the worst-case scenario is that a more rigorous data-centric approach will refine their instincts and actions to drive the best overall business outcomes. This is Data Leadership at its finest!

MAKE-AN-IMPACT! The initial push is crucial, because without it we don't get started at all. Nearly as important, but receiving far less attention, is the second push, and the one after that, and the one after that…

Sustaining efforts and building momentum over time requires the right combination of appropriate targets, virtuous cycles, and folks with motivating incentives. This is table-stakes stuff, regardless of the makeup of the actual team. But there are also patterns of what that team should start to look like as we reach the second push, and beyond.

What we will need, regardless of where they come from, is a collective band of folks that together have these powers:

- **Senior Leadership/Executive Visibility:** Able to reach top decision-makers for organizational support and resources.

- **Business Strategy:** Understand organizational vision so that potential business outcome differentials align with strategic objectives.

- **Marketing/Sales:** Able to generate support for implementing potential business outcome differentials.

- **Business Process/Operations:** Know the detailed workings of the organization so that potential business outcome differentials are feasible and implementable.

- **Data Analysis:** Able to turn raw data into meaningful insights that will create business outcome differentials.

- **Technology/Database:** Can prepare data via technology systems so that analysis can be performed.

The above are not ordered by importance, but loosely grouped in such a way that if we have three people in our data team, for example, it will be more likely that one person does the first two, the second the next two, etc. But remember, just as every organization is a little bit different, so are data teams and the skills of the individuals within them. We will need to adjust accordingly!

While we Data Leaders can make a lot happen on our own, we will inevitably need more help. Like the more functional skills that we have spent so much time talking about, leadership help can also take many different forms. Before we start our search for more Data Leaders, it is important to determine what our "asks" of them will be. Useful leadership help tends to be busy, so we are going to need to be prepared to make a strong pitch.

The most *common* ask is for resources (i.e., money and people's time) to help get our data initiatives off the ground. The most *important* ask is to get help engaging with people throughout the organization to understand why data is so important and valuable to the firm, and how what we are doing addresses it.

This presumes, of course, that we have already identified something to do that is important and valuable to the firm. If we have not yet reached that point, the efforts in reaching out to other folks will need to take a more inquisitive approach.

MAKE-AN-IMPACT! Instead of prescribing what their roles will be, we will look to them for insights on what they and others could do differently if they had more capable Data Analytics.

Note the difference between this type of inquiry and simply asking what kind of data capabilities they want. This is another example of how the questions we ask must track to maximizing Data Value.

The leadership help we get in defining the mission may not be the same as that which will help us most in getting there. Executive Vice Presidents can be excellent guides on the capabilities that will be most beneficial throughout the organization—but they operate at such an abstracted level of detail that beyond a supportive email or statement they can only help so much.

When getting an organization's data efforts off the ground, director-level folks are golden. They have connections to the executive suite, but still have operational responsibilities— and direct reports who tend to be experts in their specific areas.

MAKE-AN-IMPACT! In a large organization in the early days of Data Leadership, focus on directors and their direct reports to build the critical mass needed to get off the ground.

This is not to say others at higher and lower levels are unimportant to the success of Data Leadership. They are certainly important—just less so in the earliest days when most of the organization is blissfully unaware of how much Data Analytics will change everything.

This brings up the biggest obstacle standing in the way of maximizing Data Value: managing organizational change. People are generally change-averse, and even once you manage to break down the walls of initial resistance, there is only so much change the people of an organization can handle at once. Data people tend to get all excited about everything they can do to change things for the better, and it ends up overwhelming everybody else.

It's helpful to think of everybody else as potential clients for our data efforts. These folks do not owe us Data Leaders anything. They have jobs to do, and it is up to us to show them that we can help improve their lives. This assumes that we have a realistically executable plan on how to improve their lives.

MAKE-AN-IMPACT! Be prepared to do some marketing and sales, and do not expect an "if-we-build-it-they-will-come" approach to be enough.

The people on the front lines of our organizations are often the closest to our external customers, and also to the data we talk so much about. Business operations are where much of our data is born, and the folks creating it probably know more about it than anybody else. If we ever hope to establish better Data Quality, for example, that path runs right through operations. So why not get them involved early? This could take the form of asking them to complete surveys, or even giving them a spot on our core data team.

There is a TV show that became popular in recent years called *Undercover Boss*. The premise is that company CEOs pretend to be junior employees, and hilarity ensues. The "boss" is usually pretty bad at the lower-level job, and then learns an important lesson in the end. There are usually hugs, and crying is often involved. It's all quite formulaic. But why is it such a popular show? It's because people are so desperate to be heard by leadership that they will spend their free time watching a show that gives them a glimpse of what that might be like. Also it's pretty entertaining to watch silly executives fail at basic tasks and then get all emotional about it.

This further highlights a common disconnect between management and what is really happening in their businesses. I've always been a bit in awe of those CEOs who actually work their way up from the mail room (or comparable low-level job) and after 30 years make it to the top. To have that kind of tenacity and dedication is a quality we just do not see enough of anymore. Hopefully, these leaders do not forget where they came from, and continue to remember what it was like on the front lines.

For the rest of us who change jobs much more frequently, we will not usually have the direct experience that perfectly overlaps with our operational folks—and to be fair, even the homegrown CEO didn't personally hold every job. We must try to directly elicit as much information as possible, and the rest of the time we must rely on our own personal experience as a proxy, trying to relate these to many more situations than those we've had ourselves.

One experience I often look back on was when I was working at a country club halfway house the summer after my freshman year of college. The halfway house is where we made snacks and sandwiches for golfers that are halfway through their 18-hole round—not to be confused with a halfway house that helps ease the transition between prison and freedom. One golfer who had ordered a hot dog, after signing his slip to pay, asked me if I had touched his hot dog. I explained that yes, I did touch his food long enough to wrap it up. He then, without another word, threw out the hot dog and left. The thought that a kitchen worker may have touched his food was enough to get him to play nine more holes of golf without the nourishment he needed for top performance—though the six beers he also purchased would hopefully keep him properly hydrated.

I learned at that moment that some people have unreasonable expectations, and sometimes there will be nothing we can do to fix it. I also learned that some people will always think they are better than others, and I resolved never to be one of those people.

MAKE-AN-IMPACT! Everybody has something to teach us if given the opportunity. As much as we might know about something, there will be another person with a deeper understanding, or a specialized perspective that shines new light on the topic.

As data people, our role can be distilled to "illuminating truth for others to see." Think of it as lighting up a sculpture in a museum. What happens when we shine a light at a statue? The directly illuminated parts become much more clear, but shadows are created in other places—and this contrast can cause unintended consequences. People may perceive elements that are not actually there.

Casting light from one direction will never completely light up a statue. We need at least three or four sources of light surrounding it, arranged at different heights. We must account for shadows and different viewing angles, and attempt to give others a perfect representation of what is real.

This sounds similar to our data challenges, right? We must attempt to present an objective picture through subjective viewpoints. Our shadows are not from how the light appears from where we are standing, but from people's bias and interpretation of the data they consume. Addressing this is a task that, as it scales, will rely on the entire Data Leadership Framework to be applied thoughtfully but kept in balance with ever-greater impacts.

In the early days, however, we must first find help from those who can identify the truth that we will ultimately need to illuminate. This is why data scientists are such a hot commodity these days—they are seen as the oracles that can lead us from data chaos to Data Value. This is not to be confused with Oracle, the awesomely-named company that has a mixed track-record of delivering on said promise.

The title "data scientist" is becoming almost as prevalently used and misunderstood as "Big Data." People seem to use it to refer to anything that is difficult and has something to do with data. This is too broad, and not very useful, so we will clarify:

A data scientist is a person who performs sophisticated statistical analyses across large, disperse data sets—and has the computer programming ability to transform these analyses into algorithms with wide-ranging applicability to an organization. These math and computer skillsets, when wielded together, result in tremendous potential Data Value. One person can do with data the equivalent of taking raw carbon and turning it into a perfectly cut diamond ring—impressive!

The downside is that this is not a particularly scalable process. We hear data scientists referred to as "unicorns"—and whether or not that is an apt description is debatable. But what is not debatable is the fact that if we want to operationalize data scientists' outcomes (effectively creating diamonds from raw carbon), we are not going to be able to staff the data mines with a herd of unicorns. So if we're lucky enough to have any high-performing data scientists in our midst, we must focus on amplifying their artisanal capabilities through operational integration.

MAKE-AN-IMPACT! We must build supporting competencies to transform Data Science prototypes into functioning Data Value systems that will serve our businesses needs at scale.

The worst thing we can do is ask the data scientists to do this themselves. It would be like asking a shoe cobbler to run Nike's operations. The skill sets required are mostly divergent, though there will certainly be places where the cobbler's expert knowledge and advice would help inform the design of the scaled-up processes and systems.

To appropriately lead the charge to improve an organization's data-driven abilities, we need a Data Leader who can communicate with the data scientists, the broader technology teams, the business executives, all departments, the front-line workers—and knows a lot about Data Management, governance, and the whole data world. We might just need a Chief Data Officer!

The Ridiculous Chief Data Officer

A Chief Data Officer (CDO) is a newer title that has enjoyed increasing popularity in the business community generally, but especially in Data Management and Data Governance circles. Data folks seem to interpret this as a coming-out party for what we do—but it may speak just as loudly to the fact that people recognize there is a problem, but still haven't agreed on an approach to solve it.

Note that some organizations choose to call this new role a Chief Analytics Officer (CAO) or Chief Digital Officer (also CDO). Some of the detailed responsibilities vary with the emphasis connoted by the title, but the gist of the role is effectively the same: maximizing Data Value creation at an organizational-level. For our purposes, we're going to use Chief Data Officer (CDO) as the catch-all for all of these titles.

The role and level of the CDO is widely varied from organization to organization. Many so-called CDO have no direct reports. How is someone with no people on their team going to be a "chief" of anything? This sounds like someone with a role without a proper balance between empowerment and accountability. If people filling these CDO roles are willing to accept impossible jobs, then it hurts the entire community.

We must balance pragmatism with our need to work with what we have. If they want to call us "Chief Data Officer" but not give us the tools to do that job, we must insist on something more appropriate for right now, like "Data Leadership Advocate." That way, we have a title that reflects our responsibility (empowerment + accountability), and after we knock that out of the park, we will have room for title growth as our team and scope-of-influence continue to expand.

We definitely need something that looks like a Chief Data Officer—someone whose job it is to tirelessly maximize Data Value for an organization by overseeing the many Data Management-related activities that must work in tandem. This is less about the specific title, and more about how to fulfill these vast responsibilities within the context of a complex organization.

Data people love to have the same conversation over and over again. Attend a data conference and we are inevitably confronted with questions like "What skills are necessary to be a good CDO?" and "Where should the Chief Data Officer report in an organization?"

It's as if the CDO were some sort of data superhero. Where do these mysterious beings come from? Do Chief Data Officers come from project management, technical teams, or a planet in a neighboring galaxy? Do their mythical powers derive from magic or a terrible science experiment?

We want our CDOs to be knowledgeable executives, accomplished managers, profound business minds, and brilliant technologists. Yes, that sounds fantastic! In the real world we have individuals, all of whom have unique career stories. They have strengths, weaknesses, and resume gaps. We can talk of ideals, but we must hire real people who will never quite fit perfectly.

MAKE-AN-IMPACT! A good CDO candidate will be able to help our business use data to get better at what it does. Find the best person at doing that, and where they came from will be less important than where they will help us go.

Let's assume we have a CDO candidate identified. This is often a new position in the organization, whose responsibilities are clearly important, but cross over many functions that we already have in our businesses. It is often a nontrivial exercise to figure out how to fit the role in organizationally.

An early question we must ask our organizations is whether CDOs should report to IT or the business. A common response among data professionals is: "Of course the CDO should report to the business! Don't be silly! The data is too important to be left to IT's crazy ways!"

This kind of groupthink reaction is not only scary, but it fails to fully consider the resume requirements of being a CDO alongside the empowerment and accountability balance that they will need to successfully perform their role. Let's break it down a little more carefully:

- Does data need technology to be made useful? (Yes.)

- Does IT do technology stuff for your company? (Yes.)

- Does the business rely on IT to support other essential business functions? (Yes.)

- So the Chief Data Officer should obviously report to the business and not IT? (???)

Why are we even having this conversation?

MAKE-AN-IMPACT! IT is overwhelmingly the most logical place for the Chief Data Officer to reside.

This is a bold statement. It may even elicit a visceral negative response inside those of us who know for a fact if we put the role of the CDO inside IT, the CDO will be less effective in our particular organizations. Why is that? Have we completely lost faith in our technology people to be a trusted part of the business?

Well, in a word, yes.

MAKE-AN-IMPACT! This entire dialog about the CDO reporting anywhere other than IT is because IT has lost its relevance to the business.

Our technology organizations have been failing the business for a long time. It's embedded in the culture and language of IT operations. For example, "requirements gathering" connotes a one-directional flow of information from the business to IT. It's like a Taco Bell drive through: "I'll have the Office 365 Burrito please, and 2 CRM Soft Tacos." Coming right up! What kind of sauce would you like?

IT has been trained to focus their energy on assembling outputs from their core ingredients on request. They get talked at by the business, and then do whatever necessary to keep from being yelled at. Not being yelled at is a surprisingly good motivator.

When IT becomes overwhelmed with requests, things slow down, and eventually they start to say no. Relations between the business and IT degrade, Shadow IT pops up, and everybody is angry with each other. Something big must be done.

Enter the Chief Data Officer. Here is a technology-ish person who cares! Who "gets" the business, and has empathy for their needs. Certainly the CDO will be a real partner who will get it right this time—even though they are often given a minuscule team with a vague mandate, and no real authority beyond that. What could go wrong?

We are watching history repeat itself. We've been down this road before. This is why we created the Chief Information Officer (CIO) role decades ago! The Chief Technology Officers (CTOs) of the world became too focused with the internal departmental challenges of producing and operating capable technology solutions on behalf of their businesses. The CTOs under-invested in their business strategy and alignment responsibilities because those outputs were harder to measure, and probably seemed less important than the technical challenges of running IT. Or maybe they were simply trying to get people to stop yelling at them.

Over time, it became clear that, in many organizations, IT had lost its way by seemingly focusing on things that the business couldn't care less about. To restore the business-first focus of the IT department, the CIO role was created to oversee all organizational information assets without being operationally responsible for all of the technology itself. So what happened is that over time, the CIOs under-invested in their business strategy and alignment responsibilities, and have become too focused on the day-to-day operations of technology development and support.

And today the cycle repeats, but instead of putting the Chief Data Officer as the head of the IT group, they are being put in other business units—entirely removed from oversight of the technology systems necessary to achieve Data Value. This is treating symptoms without addressing the real underlying problems, and it is not going to solve the organizational challenges we've always faced. To break the cycle we are going to need to fix the real problem.

The Ridiculous CIO

CIOs need to be actual C-level executives. This means a strategic business function with a meaningful impact to the success of the company. By necessity, it is a role with a profit-and-loss responsibility. Success at the C-level requires a measurable contribution, and that must be a balanced one. A cost-center head cannot be an effective C-level executive.

MAKE-AN-IMPACT! Organizations need to be evaluating why CIOs are not living up to their expectations instead of creating new C-level positions set up to fail in new ways.

But creating poor positions is not the only problem. An even bigger challenge is that we have few truly-qualified candidates to fill these roles, whether we call them CIOs or CDOs. Remember, the current engagement model of our technology organizations is that of manning take-out windows: gathering requirements and delivering projects with no expectation of creativity or problem solving beyond technical specifications. This has led to a world where we have few strategically-aligned technology professionals available to perform true business executive CIO roles.

Despite this, CIOs are everywhere. Most are performing incomplete functions with incomplete skills, delivering incomplete value. We must stop filling our CIO positions with technology directors or CTO-equivalents. Our Chief Data Officers aren't real C-level positions unless they are in lieu of a CIO, and our data systems builders should absolutely report up to the CDO, if they exist.

MAKE-AN-IMPACT! A CDO's domain of responsibility is a subset of the CIO's, not a separate one. But when the CIO is actually a technology operations person with the wrong title, this relationship becomes less obvious.

What we need are better CIOs. What we need are people who are asked to be strategic parts of the business from early in their careers, not just when they reach the top and wonder why they don't really have a seat at the table. We need to completely rethink the role of technology and data throughout our organizations. These are good ideas, but they are also big, sweeping changes that we will need years to achieve. What can be done now?

First we must learn from within. Data systems development and operations have not yet embraced the collaborative techniques the applications side of technology have created. Agile, DevOps, Continuous Testing/Deployment, NoSQL, cloud technologies—all of these can begin to help us understand how to react more nimbly.

These are technology-driven innovations that we can build upon from within our IT and data groups. The greater challenge is rebuilding a healthy relationship between IT and the business. This is where there is no secret formula.

MAKE-AN-IMPACT! Building IT into a critical business capability requires executive sponsorship, strong leadership throughout, and most importantly, empathy.

We need to want to come together to make our organizations better. In the end, we should stop caring so much about the Chief Data Officer. We shouldn't pretend that this singular position fundamentally changes anything by itself. We must address the real problems that cause our organizations to break down.

Let's find ways to drive business innovation with data. Invest in that however we can, in any way it works for our business. Our competitors are certainly doing the same. Our customers will tell us the path we must take to be successful. We should listen to them. Adjust. Improve. Listen some more.

The Ridiculous Consultants

When thinking about the many different roles and functions we need internally, it can become overwhelming. We may feel alone and confused. Fear not, as there are plenty of folks out there who would also like to help us. They are consultants. And they can let us tap into a wealth of experience and skills that can be difficult to obtain from within our organizations.

Consultants spend a lot of time and energy becoming and staying knowledgeable in their particular areas of expertise. Well, good ones do at least. Mediocre consultants focus less on building their own capabilities, and more on convincing whomever they can that they are knowledgeable. Watch out for those that claim to know it all, but cannot really back it up.

The wisest among us recognize through their wisdom how little they actually know. Data Leadership is so broad that it's perfectly reasonable to seek help with specific functions or defining an overall strategy.

MAKE-AN-IMPACT! As we learn more and realize how much bigger all of this is than we originally thought, it is reasonable to want some help with it. This is exactly why consultants exist, and why they can help us—if we know how to use them.

Consultants have a binary existence. They are either billing (charging clients for services), which makes everybody happy because it brings in dollars to keep the consulting firm running—or they are not billing, which means they are using that time to learn new tricks and trying desperately to get back to billing before they get fired or the business folds. It can be a painfully cyclical process, far removed from the cliché images portrayed by TV shows like House of Lies.

It is important to think about the consulting business model to understand the incentives that motivate consultants. If we understand their motivations, then we will be able to appropriately assess our interactions with them—and evaluate the worthwhileness of proposed engagements.

Consultants want to be billable, and consulting firms want to have their people be as billable as possible—this is how the money gets made. It's a reasonable business model, but it causes some inherent conflicts of interest related to serving clients effectively. When the consultant's help is no longer required, their desire to remain billable may be in conflict with their client's needs.

Ask any consultant about the importance of "follow-on work" (aka "after work"). This is the foundation of the traditional consulting business model—an initial strategy engagement followed by years of full-time implementation work by a couple dozen lower-level associates raking in higher-level fees! Greed is good! Money-money-money!

This model is disgusting. Nowhere in there is even a thought about what the client actually needs. Consultants who make it all about themselves may find ways to make a lot of money, but they will never earn it.

MAKE-AN-IMPACT! This kind of consultant has never seen a potential client that doesn't desperately need what they are selling. To paraphrase the old saying: If you are selling hammers, everything is a nail.

Given the broad scope of Data Leadership, every organization may need some additional help, but the path forward does not require consultants. The catch is that without consultants, there is an enormous amount of learning and experience we still need to get from somewhere—either by growing it internally or hiring folks with those skills (who would otherwise likely be consultants themselves). Regardless, some amount of investment will be required, and most organizations will find that occasionally bringing in some help from consultants will be the best way to get the extra capabilities we need.

An approach some organizations use to find external help is the Request for Proposal (RFP). This is where the client organization creates a typically lengthy document that outlines everything they would like to see in an upcoming project. Consulting firms then bid on the project, or pieces of the project, and then the client organization reviews and selects the proposal and firm they like best.

RFPs are particularly common in the public sector and with large companies that are going to be spending lots of money on an upcoming project. These RFPs take a significant amount of effort to write on the client side, and a significant amount of work on the consulting firm side to respond—and with a relatively small chance for any individual consulting firm of winning the work.

This leads to some unintended consequences. In most RFPs, the selection criteria is dominated by pricing, typically alongside a check-the-box assessment of whether the proposal satisfies the particular requirements of the RFP. This leads to the lowest-cost provider having a built-in advantage over more capable, but more costly proposals.

MAKE-AN-IMPACT! Consulting firms with higher service quality levels tend to perform worse in RFPs because these firms are less likely to cut corners to reduce costs, and therefore less likely to win bids overly biased toward the lowest cost solution.

Additionally, there is a phenomenon in any bidding scenario known as the "winner's curse." This means that whichever firm bids the lowest is the most likely to have made a significant mistake in estimating the resources they will need to complete the project successfully. Because they were willing to quote the lowest price, the firm must have some combination of a willingness to accept lower margins, a more efficient delivery model, or a differing assessment of the project itself.

This implies that the firm most likely to win an RFP by virtue of low pricing will probably end up losing money on the project. Unless, of course, the consultant finds ways to cut corners in delivery or add scope (and cost) to the total project. Sadly, some firms specialize in doing just this. They will underbid the project to win it, and then rely on change requests and additional fees to make their money. This creates an environment where the best consulting firms will often avoid RFPs altogether because the low likelihood of it being a good ROI for them in the end.

These are risks and tradeoffs that arise with RFPs, but they can be mitigated. If we are in an organization setting up and evaluating RFPs, we should try to base the selection criteria on a more balanced value concept, rather than incomplete pricing criteria. Instead of passively posting the RFP on a website where people need to hunt it down, let's identify a number of known high-quality firms and actively invite them to create a proposal. And the easier for the consulting firms to participate, the more qualified responses we'll get.

Finally, we should establish reasonable ways to handle new information that arises during the project, or may not have been completely explained in the original RFP. Incentivize vendor performance to encourage delivery excellence. And remember, though it is perfectly laudable to seek good value, we will inevitably get what we pay for.

MAKE-AN-IMPACT! We should not try to take advantage of our consulting partners, and then we will be justified in demanding they do not try to take advantage of us.

However the consulting selection process happens, whenever we choose to use consultants there are some things we can do to encourage the most productive outcomes.

First, if the proposal is for a strategy project that includes an assessment and corresponding recommendations, we should be extra careful. Most consultant recommendations will include follow-on work for that firm, with varying levels of justification. We must insist that consultants make recommendations that are not predicated on their continued involvement. It is fine to have the option to continue with the consultant's help, but we must also have a viable path forward without them.

Second, if the deliverables are something like a PowerPoint deck and executive read-out presentation, we are in danger of the deliverables becoming "shelf-ware." This is when a well-intentioned consulting project was completed, but there were no additional resources available for the recommended follow-on implementation efforts. The deliverables become stale over time, and when the client organization is ready to move forward they need to do another strategic assessment to understand how things have changed since the last one.

Organizations have done this multiple times without ever getting to the real work of fixing things! The way to mitigate shelf-ware is to first line-up more resources than just what is required by the assessment—and we should be committed to take action regardless of how scary the recommendations turn out. Let's gain agreement on an ongoing engagement model with any external entities from the very beginning. It can benefit everyone to move away from a project/transactional relationship to one with a deeper commitment to long-term improvements—and one where the real business impacts (good or bad) are shared with the consulting partners who helped create them. This will only work if there is trust between client and consultant, and that takes time, too.

This is a demanding approach, and one that may chase away those firms that have solved for the price-biased RFP approach. The consultants who remain may be expensive, because it is not easy to become good enough to sign up for this kind of arrangement. These consultants also tend to be busy, as they tend to have many clients that will never let them go. These are the kind of partners we want alongside us on our Data Value journey.

MAKE-AN-IMPACT! As important and central as people are to data success, it would be wrong to think that technology is less important. It's really about balance, just like so much of what we've covered so far.

In the Data Leadership Framework we've discussed how new technologies may capture people's attention, and that we will need to acknowledge that if we want to gain support for our essential, but perhaps-less-inspirational endeavors. Because many of us have limited opportunities to learn about the tools and technologies our companies have not yet adopted, the next chapter provides some background and basic information on the latest new technologies with which all Data Leaders should have some familiarity.

13   DATA LEADERSHIP TECHNOLOGIES TO KNOW

Data without technology is like spaceflight without technology: we won't be getting very far. Technology evolves quickly, and has reached the point where nobody can keep track of all the latest trends or understand everything that might be useful to our organizations.

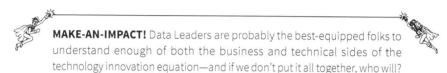

MAKE-AN-IMPACT! Data Leaders are probably the best-equipped folks to understand enough of both the business and technical sides of the technology innovation equation—and if we don't put it all together, who will?

Thinking about new technology solutions is a risky proposition, because without discipline we can fall into the trap of becoming too product-focused. Technology at its best is a pure amplifier of everything else we have talked about in this book—it does not solve our problems for us. At its worst, technology adds so much noise and inefficiency to our data efforts that it sabotages everything we might attempt to do. As long as we keep this power versus risk dynamic in mind as we walk this virtual showcase, we should be okay.

Big Data

I am begrudgingly including this topic, even though the concept of Big Data is simply an umbrella under which many capable technologies fall. There is no such thing as a pure Big Data solution. If a vendor salesperson claims that they are selling a Big Data product, be skeptical. There's a strong chance that (ironically) the underlying technology is getting a little outdated, or they are oversimplifying the capabilities of what they are trying to sell.

Either way, we should never see a box on a workflow or architecture diagram labeled Big Data. It simply doesn't mean enough without additional context. But since Big Data has been thrown around as a term for quite a while now, before we move on to more actionable things, we should make sure we understand some of its background.

For the last approximately fifty years, we have had different ways of storing, accessing, and aggregating data in databases and other mechanisms.

MAKE-AN-IMPACT! Big Data represented the size, speed, or complexity of data beyond what the current systems at any time could reasonably handle. It was a constantly moving target, making it a lousy point of reference.

We have now reached a point where we can scale without an effective limit. Terabytes, please—child's play! Petabytes, no problem. Even exabytes can be handled with today's systems. Need to look up how big an exabyte is? Quick answer, it is more than we have. A slightly longer answer based on what I found in Wikipedia is that an exabyte is approximately 15,000 times more information than the words in all of the books ever written, including this one. It's a million terabytes. It is unbelievably *Big Data*.

MAKE-AN-IMPACT! This is why the conversation about Big Data is now over: we can handle anything. Any amount of data we can possibly obtain can be elegantly managed by today's data systems. It may be expensive, but it absolutely can be done.

Now we need to figure out which particular technology tools will be most helpful to solve our actual challenges.

Public Cloud

The single most important factor contributing to the exponential growth in our ability to handle very large data sets is the decoupling of access to computing power from the need to manage physical infrastructure. In simpler terms, the advent of public cloud.

Big, smart companies realized years ago that they could operate large data centers with better economies of scale than individual companies—and if they created an effective interface into the resulting computing capabilities, other companies would be willing to pay for it.

This was established at Amazon Web Services from the early days of their retail organization, where Amazon was built using these same frameworks. Exciting times for a burgeoning business when starting with a marquee client from day one—and that client is also you! As prescient as that original idea was, nobody could fully imagine the kinds of dynamic new technologies and design patterns that would grow from the early days of AWS.

Today the cloud offers the ability to scale processing down to responding to individual micro-events, with à la carte pricing available down to fractions of a second! Buying that ETL server that sits idle for 18 hours a day maybe seems a bit suboptimal now, doesn't it?

Here are five reasons to consider embracing a cloud-first strategy:

Instant Infrastructure Availability

Anyone who has built technology systems for any amount of time has had this happen. Our project finally gets the green light from the business, the finance people, and anybody else who likes to say no, and what happens?

We wait.

Well, actually first we go through the hassles of ordering the new data center equipment, and then we wait for it to be processed, shipped, installed, configured, provisioned, and then we might be able to start working with it. Typically weeks, if not months, of hassle and delay.

In the cloud, the high-level process is roughly the same, except the steps all happen through a console on our PC. And it takes about five minutes from start to finish.

And that's for planned infrastructure availability. Unplanned infrastructure availability takes the same amount of time once we have made the decision to do it. We'll want to have some internal controls in place to keep people from going nuts with it, but that's a problem worth solving to cut weeks or months off of every acquisition of new computing power.

After all, isn't this how things should be? The hard part should be strategically deciding what to do—everything else is just friction between the potential value of an opportunity and realizing the value from it. Comparing it to the old ways of procuring infrastructure, the cloud makes traditional data center supply chain delays seem nothing short of ridiculous.

Infinite Scalability

Speaking of ridiculous, at various points in previous, unenlightened, on-premises stops in my career I would be building a new database environment and realize I'd need new server on which to run my creation. I'd put together a business case asking for some money, eventually get approval, and then it would be time to order the equipment.

Inevitably, I'd be contacted by somebody in a deeper, darker IT cave than the one in which I lived, and they would ask me the question I hated most: "So what specs do you need on that server?"

As a database-centric geek, I knew I wanted something good, but I had no idea how my database performance translated into the server specifications. Knowing I'd only have one chance to buy the machine I needed, I wasn't going to err on the side of underpowered or undersized. So I'd get the biggest, fastest, most expensive option that didn't exceed my budget.

And the IT purchaser couldn't have cared less—they just wanted their headache (me) to go away. The net result is that companies with on-premises data center equipment probably spent more than they needed to on servers, but their databases had plenty of processing headroom. But what was the alternative—accidentally get too weak of a machine? Doom the project before one piece of software is written or applied? No thank you.

MAKE-AN-IMPACT! One might argue that the misalignment of excess computing power acquired versus what was actually necessary is just one more intrinsic cost of living in the old data center world.

Now, with the cloud, we can manage infrastructure resources the way we develop code: trial and error. See if it works; if not, then make some changes. The scalability of the cloud is so limitless, it enables entirely new ways of working with infrastructure. We can start with our best guess, and then iteratively measure performance and change the underlying capabilities on the fly.

This is especially helpful in new environments that may receive little traffic initially, but will grow in usage over time. We can even configure environments to scale automatically, based on usage metrics that are natively tracked. But the most exciting extension of unlimited scalability is not how big we can grow it, but how small!

New Development Approaches

One of the latest innovations in cloud technologies are microservices and serverless computing. Serverless computing essentially allows the resources to exist only as long as we need to run a small application. Microservices applications typically do a discrete task, like land an individual data file into a database table.

The magic is in how they are instantiated. Sure, we can schedule them to run at set times, but that misses the point. The beauty of microservices is that they are designed to be event-driven. Cloud service providers have developed mechanisms that watch for specific conditions to occur, like a file being saved to disk, and then fire up the microservices applications that are ready to respond to these conditions.

This allows for much greater variability in how we process data. ETL should long ago have moved away from rigid processing structures and once-a-day batches.

MAKE-AN-IMPACT! With microservices and serverless computing as a backbone, we can change everything about how we process data and start breaking down the time and complexity barriers that cause delays between data being available and the business being able to act on it.

Just think: now we can truly build iteratively with data! As business requirements evolve, so can our technical approach, in tandem with our underlying hardware. In a pay-what-we-use model, we have perfect elasticity in keeping and enhancing what works while discarding the less effective approaches. The bottleneck returns to where it should be:

on the ability of the business to make decisions, and the skills of the people who carry out those decisions.

Unparalleled Power

Cloud technologies unlock capabilities that were recently fantasy. An individual business can plug into effectively infinite computing power, changing resource allocations in constant response to its evolving needs.

The most exciting aspect is that we shouldn't need to wait weeks or months to make new analytics capabilities available to the business. Turnaround times can be as short as minutes or hours for tasks that used to take much longer. The power of the cloud enables us to implement fully-interactive, Data Warehouse-driven solutions in the time it once took to deliver a basic report.

MAKE-AN-IMPACT! To realize the potential of the cloud, we need to adopt new methodologies and train our people to interact differently, as real partners.

Business and technology must solve problems together, iteratively, with the impact to the business always top of mind. Whether we choose to adopt a well-defined Agile Scrum approach, or simply change reporting structures and leave it up to individual managers, we must learn to operate in a new way.

It's like the discovery of nuclear energy. Cloud technologies are that powerful in the data and computational area. As nuclear energy did for submarines, cloud technologies can be harnessed to provide businesses power that fundamentally changes what they can accomplish. Similarly, without proper controls and governance, things can rapidly get out of hand.

These are the kinds of challenges we want in our businesses. All the power we could ever use, with a model that allows us to start small, experiment, and build on top of what works. This leads to the bottom line: a cost/benefit ratio possibly higher than any other investment our businesses could make.

Off-the-charts Cost/Benefit

Many organizations have recently adopted a cloud-based, columnar storage/massively-parallel processing Data Warehouse product. This product has all the scalability capabilities of the cloud, but can be had for about $1,000 per terabyte per year, and starts at about $250 a month all-in. It wasn't too long ago that the only way into this kind of technology was a dedicated data center appliance, with a $100,000+ price tag before we'd even turn it on.

Because the technology is so inexpensive at small scale, we can do a pilot project with real data in just a couple of weeks from start to end. When is the last time any data-related project with a measurable business impact was done in two weeks? Most projects can't even be scoped in two weeks! Therein lies the opportunity—and the challenge. What we've glimpsed at here scratches the surface of what the cloud is, and how it can impact our world of data and analytics.

In every industry there are players seizing the potential of the cloud and upending the old institutions that once seemed immune to competitive threats. In the short-term, it may feel easier to ignore the world changing around us, and seek comfort in the warm glow of big servers in big rooms with big price tags. But that decision may erode the competitiveness of our businesses to the point of no return. The time is now to decide whether our companies will be bold and join the disruptors, or avoid the cloud and hope the status quo will somehow keep us competitive!

MAKE-AN-IMPACT! The decisions we make today about our technology infrastructure will have greater impact on the future competitiveness of our businesses than they ever have before.

But before we move on to technologies beyond the cloud, we need to address a dangerous falsehood being promoted as cloud by certain technology companies that will slap a fancy label on anything that will drive sales. We must learn to distinguish clever marketing from real innovation, especially when it comes to the hype that currently surrounds the cloud.

There is No Such Thing as Private Cloud

Free lunch. Unicorns. Automatic faucets that work.

None of these actually exist.

Neither does the private cloud. Private cloud is intended to mimic the public cloud, but resides within customers' data centers, whether truly on-premises or in shared co-located data centers.

MAKE-AN-IMPACT! So-called "private cloud" provides similar interface mechanisms of the public cloud, but provides none of the actual benefits of the real (public) cloud.

Private cloud is sold as the best of both worlds. It claims to give the customer all of the control they desire, with most of the benefits of public cloud.

These claims are simply untrue.

Let's break it down:

Power—NO!

Private cloud implies that the computing hardware is owned, or is fully leased, and resident in a customer data center. So the customer has access to the purchased power, no more and no less—the way it already is in a fully on-premises solution.

Cost—NO!

Private cloud requires the same high-cost structures of on-premises solutions, because it actually is an on-premises solution. Customers may even need more personnel because of the added overhead to support the cloud-like interfaces.

Scalability—NO!

Private cloud customers have access to what hardware they have. If they want more, they need to procure more, find data center space, wire the racks, install the hardware, provision access, ensure security, etc.

Security—NO!

Private cloud customers are in charge of their own fate. In a world where thousands of organizations fall victim to ransomware on a long-ago deprecated OS, doing security is not a core competency for most organizations.

Flexibility—NO!

Private cloud provides some flexibility-like behavior on the micro-scale, so long as the capabilities have already been built previously, the computing capacity exists, and the interface to those capabilities have been sufficiently developed. But this is "fake" flexibility: building and paying for excess capacity in order to have the illusion of flexibility is not actual flexibility. It is inefficiency posing as flexibility.

Speed to Delivery—NO!

Private cloud has none of the above benefits of public cloud, and therefore drives no actual speed to delivery. Failing fast, rapid iteration, trying out the new tools that didn't even exist yesterday—none of these are truly possible in the private cloud.

The only rational conclusion to this analysis is that private cloud is not cloud at all. Private cloud is a repackaging of the old ways with new terminology, promoted by legacy organizations that are trying to keep their cash cows relevant long past when the steaks should have been served. Do not fall prey to this clever marketing.

MAKE-AN-IMPACT! We should never use private cloud as a proof-of-concept of whether to move to public cloud. Those who do, learn nothing about the benefits of the public cloud, because private cloud provides none of those benefits.

Private cloud is not a real thing—but hybrid cloud is.

This is, in effect, cloud technology coming full-circle. In the past, because there was no other viable option, we used nearby data centers, whether owned by our organization or shared spaces owned by somebody else. Now with the cloud, we have the ability to tap into better economies of scale in massive, shared environments that may not be across the street.

But what happens when internet access is shaky, or we have a unique use case where it makes more sense to batch upload to the cloud at certain times?

What about an offshore oil rig? Internet access is likely slow or nonexistent entirely, and yet the operations of the rig likely generates a tremendous amount of data that would be useful to the parent organization. In normal business, however, the analytics needs of the rig operators likely rely most on the data that is generated locally on the rig. It wouldn't make a lot of sense to upload everything to the cloud first, would it?

How about a passenger jetliner? During every flight, the sensors embedded throughout the plane generate a lot of usage, performance, and maintenance-related data that will help analysts improve airline operations. Most of this is not particularly actionable during the flight itself. Would it make a lot of sense to try to upload via the shaky internet access planes have, or would it be more effective to wait until landing, plug in a cable, and upload everything in a fraction of the time?

Offshore oil rigs and jetliners are classic examples of the need for hybrid cloud architectures. Technologies available today are well-suited to accommodating these use cases, and illustrate that when it comes to data, no size fits all. When developing an approach to creating Data Value, what seems to work most of the time may not be the right solution for our particular situation.

Serverless and Event-Driven

The original cloud platforms focused around storage and virtualized servers, and this was good. Everybody had applications that needed to run on servers, and everybody had files that they needed to store. The benefits of the public cloud allowed organizations to move everything into the cloud with manageable amounts of revision.

As time has gone on and the systems have matured, public cloud has enabled more granular building blocks to emerge, along with managed services that take away many of the low-value tasks and tuning from the end consumer so they can focus on the higher-value design and development tasks. Databases, server clusters, web hosting, I/O throughput are just a few examples of what can be changed with a few clicks, or even automatically based on utilization.

MAKE-AN-IMPACT! We have now reached the logical limit of this evolution, where discrete code snippets are executed in response to individual events—all on computing capacity that exists only long enough to execute the code.

To understand what this means, imagine a picture is uploaded to our website, and when that happens we want to store the photo's storage location and other Metadata in a searchable NoSQL database so it can be quickly retrieved on demand. How would we architect this functionality in a traditional environment?

We would have a storage array of some sort, along with at least one server sitting ready to process anything that comes in, and then logging the information to a database that is sitting on at least one other server. This would work fine for a small or predictable throughput of files being uploaded, though to provide sufficient headroom, excess capacity would need to be allocated.

What if we needed to process bursts of an unknown number of files at any time, from one to 10,000,000? Then in a traditional architecture we would need a lot more usually-idle machinery to accommodate the processing peaks. This is where serverless shines brightest, for obvious reasons.

In a serverless, event-driven world, it does not generally matter what the throughput looks like, since processing power is allocated automatically when an event is triggered. In our example, this would instantly shift the processing bottleneck to the database—and if it were a managed database, it could identify the utilization spike, grow capacity to accommodate the burst of calls, and then when things settle down, it could shrink its throughput pipes back to a normal level. No three a.m. phone call required.

The economic impacts of perfectly elastic computing demand are awesome. This has already changed the world, and this is only the beginning! And if we ever find ourselves wondering why Netflix rarely slows down on a Saturday night when demand is spiking—now we might have a better understanding of why.

Open Source, Python, and R

This section is not really about these specific tools. It is really about the democratization of application logic. Coming off of the excitement of the cloud section, this is a fascinating complement. It comes down to this:

MAKE-AN-IMPACT! Almost nothing we create with software is truly new. Somebody has done something like it already. Somewhere, the code already (mostly) exists to solve (most) of our challenge.

This is why Open Source exists. Nothing we are trying to do is really all that unique on the back-end. Why not spend less time reinventing wheels and more time designing new vehicles? Why not build collectively, while still retaining the opportunity to capitalize on what makes our businesses truly unique?

Just like a traditional encyclopedia writer could never keep pace with Wikipedia, proprietary software development is losing ground to Open Source. Think back to Agile—we need to be flexible, fast, and deliberate in our priorities.

Python and R have become de facto standards for application development and deeper Data Science analysis, respectively. These play nicely in the Open Source space, and in Linux environments, especially. If we are data-technology proficient and want to expand our skills with a new language/skill set, a good place to start is Python and R.

So why are these in the same section as Open Source? It's because Python and R follow an Open Source model of facilitating sharing and reuse. Not unlike Linux itself, Python makes it easy to bring in external libraries with minimal code. The most common libraries are centrally-maintained, giving programmers incredible extensibility without needing to reinvent the wheel every time.

Who knows? In the coming years, Python and R may fall out of favor, but the Open Source movement is likely here to stay. The power of the community is too formidable for us to return to the old days of closed, proprietary commodity technology systems. It is simply not possible for those kinds of models to keep up anymore.

Internet of Things (IoT)

The Internet of Things (IoT) has been the next hot new thing for a while. The early days were a bit misguided, thinking that things like Twitter-enabled refrigerators would be the killer applications. That one was a bit off-the-mark, but we have recently seen an explosion of smart home devices like thermostats, security cameras, lighting, and smoke detectors.

MAKE-AN-IMPACT! Sensors are the IoT killer app. From the home improvement projects favored by nerds like me, to large-scale manufacturing and logistics sensor arrays favored by nerds like General Electric—the ability to measure fine details at massive scale has revolutionary implications.

These days we are really starting to see the Data Value side of IoT! Amazon opened the first grocery store that has no checkout counters, and now someday down the road people will ask, "What's a checkout counter?" A myriad of systems come together to drive a concept as simple as not making people waste time in a pointless line just waiting to hand over their money.

The kinds of technologies that enable simple sensory functions in individual devices can be combined to do science-fiction-like magic. Driverless cars, drones, rockets that fly to space and come back to earth to land upright, the AI sisters (Alexa, Siri, and the Google one)—and we are still in the early days!

IoT is where the incredible abilities we have built in the virtual world of computers reaches the physical world of people. Previous attempts were hampered by technology limitations, but now it is ON, and in a tremendous way. If you have an ability to get involved in it, definitely consider it.

Smart Data Lakes

Data lakes are so 2015. For a while there, everybody was super-excited about these mystical data repositories that can unify all the data that an organization might need to become awesome at Data Value creation. What characterized these early data lakes is that they pushed a concept called "schema-on-read," which means that we only worry about what makes up the data when we are trying to use the data.

This is in contrast to the more traditional Data Warehouse pattern of "schema-on-write," which wraps all of the data in structure and understanding when it enters the environment, regardless whether it is ever actually used by anybody. What's the downside of a "schema-on-write" approach? It wastes a lot of energy (i.e., cost) on structuring data that is never used to create Data Value.

To compare, what is the downside of a "schema-on-read" architecture? It's that everything is a big mess and we can't tell where the useful stuff is when we want to use it! This is the ultimate sweep-it-under-the-rug mentality, and it made for an incomplete vision of data lakes. The truth is neither schema-on-write nor schema-on-read is the right approach—the data lake design paradigm is the smart data lake.

MAKE-AN-IMPACT! Smart data lakes takes the principal benefit of the original data lakes, in being a wholesale repository for all of the data, and wraps that repository in a reasonable amount of structure and context.

By tracking the Metadata of data lake objects, we enable new design and development patterns, like decoupling Data Refinement from Data Adoption. In the past, data would be loaded into a Data Warehouse and the data would progress through several steps:

"landing -> staging -> production -> history" is a popular progression, but some may add "change data capture," "master data," "data quality," or other similar steps.

With a smart data lake we are not required to do these steps in the same database, or even at all! We can create derivatives from our source data, write them back to the smart data lake, and then use those refined versions as the jumping-off point for a multitude of downstream use cases.

This lets us use technologies perfectly suited to the tasks at hand. After all, the specific operations involved in assessing Data Quality and establishing Master Data are different than the aggregation mechanisms needed for large-scale reporting and analytics. Once we understand the dynamics of a smart data lake, it almost seems silly to manage data any other way.

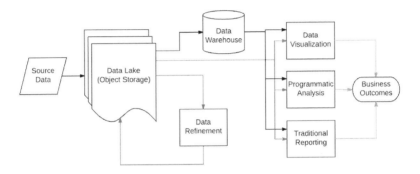

A Smart Data Lake Architecture

These have just been a few major innovations that Data Leaders must consider as we embark on our Data Leadership journey, and there are so many more to come. Although the timeliness of these observations will lessen, history will judge their relevancy. If things like public cloud and microservices do not stand the test of time, it will be as shocking as if relational databases ever went away. I won't say it is impossible, but I will say it is highly unlikely!

 MAKE-AN-IMPACT! Learning more about the innovation trends that will impact us for many years is one of the best ways for Data Leaders to ensure our own relevancy in the future.

Whether Data Leadership, or simply leadership in general, so much of what we do is about developing a vision for the future—and subsequently making it happen. We've already covered so many levels of this fundamental pattern, and we have just one topic left, and it is the final piece in making a true lasting impact on our organizations. And it starts with rethinking one of the most reviled parts of working in an office setting: projects for everything.

14   WATCH THIS

It's easy to think about projects, since they have definable beginnings and ends, along with reasonably clear objectives and expectations. The concept of data projects is appealing, but may also oversimplify what we are really trying to accomplish. On one hand, data projects are familiar coordination mechanisms that align behaviors of diverse groups of stakeholders toward a common positive outcome. On the other hand, they are finite—and frequently project sponsors mistakenly believe that when the projects are done, the Data Value story is complete.

MAKE-AN-IMPACT! One problem is that data, for better or worse, is often associated with technology—and technology projects often result in something that people can use from that point on, like a software application or a new server coming online.

Data project sponsors may assume that data works similarly, but data is far from a build-it-and-then-we're-done type of effort. Of course we will never be done with data! This should be obvious by now when we consider things like social media, the Internet of Things, Big Data, and the fact that even grandmothers have cell phones.

We need to help our organizations understand that these are just the early days before the real insanity to come—and if we are not ready to commit to data excellence for the long term, we are going to be in big trouble. The disruption that we are helping to cause in every industry is changing the way business gets done, and this will not stop any time soon. And if we want to convince people to change their ways, nothing beats a good story.

Show and Not (Just) Tell: The Eight-Second Proof-of-Concept

Let's assume we have a data initiative in mind that will create some amount of Data Value in our company. What do we do? We might think the first step is to get formal approval to do the project.

The problem is that a project means significant effort, which means providing an assessment of resource requirements, return-on-investment, and opportunity costs. That means we would need to know all of those things. If we're just getting going, we simply won't know enough detail to be persuasive with this kind of approach.

We will certainly need to get somebody's permission to get resources for a larger-scale project at some point, but there is a better way. Before attempting to formalize a larger effort, we should first establish credibility and create some initial momentum that we can build upon.

MAKE-AN-IMPACT! We need to first demonstrate a nominal amount of real Data Value before we will convince executives to open the checkbook.

The following story is real, and it reinforces one of the most important lessons of this book: that we need to stop talking about data and start making an impact. Some of the minor details have been adjusted to protect folks' privacy, but the main outcomes are what really happened.

Several years ago, I was on a consulting engagement with a significantly sized public-sector transportation organization that wanted to do more with Data Analytics. They had rolled out a new fare collection system in the prior few years, and with the new fare system came a wealth of data that the organization hadn't previously seen.

Unfortunately, the vendor of that system maintained control of all the data—and the vendor provided my client access to this data via a web-based business intelligence tool that could create reports on-demand. The fare system collected information about roughly a million rides per day, split between bus and rail services, and a typical report would be a look at total daily ride counts for each of those categories over the course of a month. This is a simple report with a total of 60 numbers (30 days x 2 numbers/day).

In the legacy reporting system, this simple report would take 42 minutes to run, but would fail 60 percent of the time. Abysmal, by any modern standard. It seemed the vendor was running this business intelligence environment in the same database where many other core operational tasks were taking place (a big no-no). This poor performance was consistent throughout the data environment, and earlier attempts at data replication and direct access had not resulted in any meaningful improvements.

My team had been invited by the client to help solve their Data Analytics challenges, and we quickly determined that with this reporting environment it would be impossible to achieve our goals. The real problem we now faced was figuring out what to do about it.

The IT organization thought everything was fine(!), so they were not particularly interested in adding to their already-overwhelming workload. The organization as a whole did not have the funds or other resources to go purchase new hardware and put a reengineered, more robust solution in place.

We concluded that our first mission was to find a highly capable, nearly free Data Analytics technology that could be implemented without any significant assistance from IT. This admittedly seemed unrealistic, but I've always been more stubborn than sensible. Plus, it couldn't hurt to try!

I had heard a bit about public cloud technologies at that point, but had not worked much with them outside of an underpowered development environment at a prior firm. In our current circumstances, however, it seemed that the cloud might be our best hope to meet our seemingly impossible objectives. After researching options around available technologies, the team decided to do a proof-of-concept with Amazon Redshift, their petabyte-scale cloud Data Warehouse solution.

Thank goodness that somebody had the foresight to put in the fare system vendor contract that "data must be delivered from the fare system vendor to our client upon request." So, in collaboration with our client, we requested all the data.

If you ever want to see software vendors lose their minds, ask them for ALL the data. It will go something like this:

"We would like all the data." (Us)

"How quickly do you need it?" (Vendor)

"As soon as possible. Ideally today." (Us)

"Which data do you need?" (Vendor)

"All the data." (Us)

"But what time frame?" (Vendor)

"All the time frames." (Us)

"Which data points are you looking for?" (Vendor)

"All the data points." (Us)

"But we can't give you all the data." (Vendor)

"We need all the data. Would you like a copy of the contract?" (Us)

"We will call you back." (Vendor)

This conversation will happen a few times before they get it, but eventually they will realize that providing the data is what they must ultimately do to get us to stop calling. This is what they get for hoarding all of the data in the first place.

In our story, the vendor eventually acquiesced, and we began compiling a series of data extracts that would comprise the billion-plus records that we needed to recreate the database in Amazon Redshift. In total it took about a month to compile enough data to do a true apples-to-apples comparison between the legacy system and the new one.

Recall that in the legacy system, running our sample report showing a daily breakdown of bus and train rides for a month took 42 minutes, and it failed 60 percent of the time. In the new one, the same query hitting a comparable database took just eight seconds, and worked every time! Realizing what we'd done, I promptly arranged to meet with the president of the organization, who was the driving force behind our data improvement efforts—he needed to see this.

At the meeting, we explained the challenges of getting data from the legacy environment and what we did to work around it. We explained how with their legacy toolset it would be impossible to create the high-performing Data Analytics they desired. We explained that accepting poor performance in one area had made it impossible to make progress in another. And we explained that we'd found a path to fixing it all.

But the most important thing we did was demonstrate it. Instead of talking about how a new technology would help solve their challenges, we said two of the most powerful words we can say to someone we want on our side:

"Watch this."

Eight seconds later, the president of the organization gave a semi-puzzled glance at the other executive who had brought us in to help them, and then turned back to me for a moment. He paused, looked me in the eyes and said, "You can do whatever you want."

It felt almost like he had never seen someone actually demonstrate value as part of their request. And our request was so modest (please let us keep going down this path!) compared to the kinds of requests a large transit agency president would typically get. Even for those big requests, most of the time people in his position simply get a nice story with a big ask at the end:

"If we make this purchase, everything will be amazing!"

"If we do this million-dollar project, everything will be amazing!"

"If we can go back to the drawing board, everything will be amazing!"

Instead we took the initiative to test our hypothesis that this solution might work—and then we shared the data we collected in that testing along with the story we told to make it meaningful to someone with a higher-level frame of reference. Sure, we may have had to build much of it at the coffee shop across the street from the office because the domain was blocked from the network—but we got the data we needed, and those eight seconds made our point better than our best presentation deck.

MAKE-AN-IMPACT! What we did differently is show, not just tell. This is a philosophy that we as Data Leaders should try to adopt in everything we do.

People are so tired of being let down by well-intended promises that go unfulfilled. If we can give them real evidence that what they are hearing from us will be more than that, we are much more likely to get what we seek, whether it is permission, time, money, people, political support, etc.

This lesson also applies to the project management methodologies we deploy once we have "permission" to proceed. For decades, complex endeavors like Data Warehouses were built using traditional project management methodologies. Unfortunately, more than half of Data Warehouse projects fail. Too bad this isn't baseball, where we can make the Hall of Fame despite failing two-thirds of the time.

If we want to do more than get approval, and actually deliver on those promises, we need to put it all together from beginning to end.

MAKE-AN-IMPACT! While the Data Leadership Framework outlines the journey of data from potential to real value, transforming our organizations requires people to go through their own metamorphosis.

From Drowning in Waterfalls to Scrumming in Agile

So pretend we are living back in the year 2000 and we want to build a Data Warehouse to be the cornerstone of our organization's data capabilities. Our leadership gets a gleam in their eyes and commits to the multi-year journey. They assign their top project manager to run the show. Although this person may or may not know much about data warehousing, they certainly know how to run a complex project with many stakeholders.

The project manager creates a project schedule, and the early phases of this are dominated by requirements gathering and specification efforts. Seems like a reasonable approach, doesn't it? Spend some time figuring out what we want to build, then we build it, and then we unleash it upon the business and change the world!

This sounds great, but it doesn't work in the real world. In the 12 to 24 months from commencement to completion that a large Data Warehouse effort will take, how might the business change? Could there be new products or even new lines of business, or other material changes that would be missed by a requirements gathering phase that took place months before the business changes occurred? Of course there could! It happens all the time!

Even if we could require the business not to change a thing throughout the duration of a data warehousing effort, what are the chances that our initial design was exactly what would serve the stakeholder interests best over time? No chance!

 MAKE-AN-IMPACT! It is insane to think that effective Data Warehouses can be designed and built using a linear, waterfall approach. A waterfall project management approach is best suited to highly-repeatable projects with known complexities.

Like, if you need to build a commercial airplane. Most of us would agree that the safety of the end-product aircraft will be more important than anything else, and is worth the added time and resources to engineer the process accordingly. In our highly-dynamic businesses with changing requirements and unreasonable timelines, we cannot expect to be successful using this kind of approach. What we need is something more nimble, iterative, and yes, agile.

First, Agile is fundamentally a mindset, not a particular methodology. There are some core values, and the rest is up to us. Agile generally leads to a way of working in teams that tries to optimize productivity while encouraging adaptiveness and problem-solving. Let's look at the actual Agile Manifesto, available at AgileManifesto.org:

> We are uncovering better ways of developing software by doing it and helping others do it. Through this work we have come to value:
>
> **Individuals and interactions** over processes and tools
>
> **Working software** over comprehensive documentation
>
> **Customer collaboration** over contract negotiation
>
> **Responding to change** over following a plan
>
> That is, while there is value in the items on
>
> the right, we value the items on the left more.
>
> © 2001, the Agile Manifesto authors
>
> *This declaration may be freely copied in any form, but only in its entirety through this notice.*

For those who weren't previously familiar with the Agile Manifesto, it is probably a little different than expected, isn't it? Maybe we thought Agile was all about Scrum and various other suspicious project management processes that sound like they are somehow avoiding accountability.

MAKE-AN-IMPACT! Agile project management is about prioritization and responsiveness to a changing environment—and we, as Data Leaders, must be keenly aware of these things.

An Agile mindset is especially helpful when we are trying to get our organizations to devote time, dollars, and energy to something that may not have a clear and immediate payoff to the business. We know that if we do a good job in our data initiatives the impact will come, but turning that belief into reality requires perseverance, flexibility, and prioritization. The mindset is essential, but some of the practices can help, too.

In common Agile-derived approaches, tasks are arranged in terms of stories that outline capabilities that need to be delivered, with other similar constructs covering higher- or lower-level details (epics and story points, respectively). Levels of effort are typically estimated with a bit more abstraction than simply how many hours we think something will likely take. One of the key tenets of any Agile methodology is that we need a fully committed project team, including a highly available project sponsor. There are multiple flavors of Agile, with two of the most notable being Scrum and Kanban.

Scrum focuses on a daily meeting (called a "scrum") that orients the team for that day's work and provides a forum for accountability each day. The work is grouped into roughly two-week sprints that target delivering functional outputs that can be delivered to the customer.

Kanban focuses more on ongoing throughput and efficiency with less emphasis on sprints or scrums. There are many resources to learn about these techniques and others, so we won't cover them in detail here.

When you run in those circles, there is a pull that you either do Agile right (i.e., all-in), or not at all. Agile folks will warn of the dangers of "Waterscrum" and "Scrummerfall"—and they are real dangers whenever we create mutant project management methods.

Agile can get a bad rap for being directionless and unaccountable, but that is generally unfair, as strong product ownership should accomplish both. Another common criticism is that Agile tends to ignore integration with other systems and processes, but that is typically due to product ownership that is too inwardly focused. Creating user-stories related to integrations will solve this.

At the end of the day, some people just prefer to be given unrealistic waterfall schedules that always slip instead of being given tradeoffs up-front that require them to deal with the consequences of their decisions today instead of later-than-today.

MAKE-AN-IMPACT! If people are given an option to deal with their problems later instead of now, they probably will—especially when there's a small chance that the problem may go away by then.

If there is a counterpoint to the whole Agile movement, it is that is that if we have a fully committed project team, highly available project sponsor, and clear change-management process to incorporate new information, we can probably make any project management methodology work pretty well. We've witnessed such lack of rigor on both traditional waterfall projects and on Agile projects, that I believe that the chosen project management process is far less important than ensuring true transparency and adaptability to change in any way possible.

MAKE-AN-IMPACT! If we are maximizing Data Value, our teams can organize their activities however works best for them. If we are struggling to create Data Value, it may be time to try something new.

Throughout this book we have asked a lot of questions, and provided many partial answers. The sad truth is that nobody will have the complete solutions until the specific challenges and full contexts are known (not even a consultant!). But what we do have now is a good start, with some lighthouses to help us navigate our way.

Our goal was to understand the big brush strokes of what makes realizing Data Value so difficult, yet such a worthwhile pursuit. Data truly represents the future success of all businesses, and those of us who can help lead the way will impact the destiny of our organizations more than we could have ever imagined.

MAKE-AN-IMPACT! Regardless of our specific role today, whether as a junior data analyst trying to build a career, or as a senior leader trying to make our organization more competitive in its industry—Data Value and Data Leadership are crucial to our future success.

By using the coordination tools we have discussed here, along with continued study and supplementing our own personal skills with a diverse team, we will continue creating this new, data-driven reality. The one thing we know is that we have no idea really what is around the corner. Maybe we can project the next couple of years, but in general people do not have a great track record in predicting where technology improvements will lead us in the longer term.

There are certainly parallels between today's data revolution with the 1900s' Industrial Revolution. The nature of people's jobs are changing, and there is a sense of incredible potential and unlimited risk that permeates today's business climate.

None of this matters, really.

People do not experience macroeconomics firsthand. It is an aggregation, an abstraction, from the daily reality we each face. Nobody can really change the world by themselves—all we can do is change the individual circumstances of those we impact, and some people can impact more people than others. The president of the United States, typically regarded as the most powerful person in the world, only achieves that power through the cascading influence on those whom the president can impact.

So why are we talking about this? Why does this matter?

MAKE-AN-IMPACT! This matters because everything we can accomplish as Data Leaders is realized through the actions of others.

The structure of projects, getting approvals, showing not (just) telling—these are likely useful insights (if I do say so myself)—but the point is that none of them are terribly important by themselves. Remember the definition of Data Value.

MAKE-AN-IMPACT! Our ability to create meaningful outcomes is the one thing that matters, even though the tools and techniques in our repertoire will have a cascading impact on the eventual outcomes we are able to drive. But if we, as Data Leaders, can put the knowledge in these pages to use, we will save our companies and build the future we are just beginning to see in focus.

Today is an Inflection Point

Once upon a time, businesses could be successful without being data-driven. Today, shockingly, many outstanding businesses still seemingly thrive without fully embracing data. Some think they have embraced it, but a lack of something as fundamental as organized Data Governance quickly betrays that belief. They may go through the motions being data-driven, but realize little Data Value.

From my experience, these organizations still represent the majority of businesses out there. We are surrounded by gold, and everybody can see it sitting there. But Data Leaders are the only ones with the keys to open the doors that will let us bring that value inside.

Data is getting a lot of attention at the moment, and some of the technology innovations seem impossible. When SpaceX first landed a booster rocket upright on a floating barge, the video looked like bad special effects. Cars are driving themselves more and more, with full autonomy finally within reach.

Data enables truly amazing things, but at the same time our internet still seems to go out three times a day. The CFO is still complaining that the numbers on his reports do not match. We still cannot quite tell which of our employees are the most productive, or which customers contribute the most profit.

The headlines about rockets and self-driving cars capture our attention, but they are the outliers. The norm is that we are still struggling to fully unlock the potential of data in our organizations, and Data Leaders are the key. We Data Leaders understand the potential value contained in our data, the many activities necessary to turn that potential into realized value, and the balance required to maximize those real outcomes.

Further, we know that understanding these concepts is not enough. We must take action to get our businesses doing different things. This is the core of Data Value, and the role of Data Leaders is to catalyze these organizational changes.

Data Leadership is not a role for the timid. Data by itself it challenging enough—technically difficult to master, and even more arduous to talk about. Leadership is just as tough. It is not easy to get people united behind a common goal, working together to achieve extraordinary outcomes.

When we consider that everyone we work with goes home to an entire world that exists outside the office, it is amazing that we are able to gain their attention long enough to make successful businesses. Sometimes it goes sideways—after all, who hasn't had a work day dominated by personal issues? Sick kids, house problems, car trouble. Life has a way of interfering with work from time to time.

But through it all, our lives depend on others' work. As consumers, don't we want data-driven businesses serving us? Phone support that doesn't leave us on hold? Deliveries that show up on time? Emergency services that can get to us quickly?

Data Leadership is the glue that connects data and people. It leads to the goods and services upon which we all rely, every day. Data Leadership is how it all comes together to create businesses that will use data to better serve each one of us: at the office, at home, and everywhere else.

This book has started us on our Data Leadership journey, but it's just the beginning. We should remember the definition of Data Value, and orient everything we do to creating more of it. Learn from every opportunity, and try to get a little better at something every day. Find the balance that Data Leadership enables, and let nothing stop us from overcoming any challenge that stands in our way. Last but not least, try to enjoy it—being a Data Leader is among the best careers in the world.

MAKE-AN-IMPACT!

ADDITIONAL RESOURCES FROM DATAVERSITY

Digital Trade Journal

Data Management articles, blogs by industry experts, news and more.
https://dataversity.net

DATAVERSITY Conferences

Your transformation to data-driven business starts here! Learn from experts and network with peers.

https://www.dataversity.net/category/data-conferences/

DATAVERSITY Online Training

Ensure everyone on your team and in your business is ready to take their data careers to the next level.

https://training.dataversity.net/

DATAVERSITY Community

Network with peers. Engage in Data Management forums. Converse with experts. Research vendors and products.

https://community.dataversity.net/

DATAVERSITY Upcoming Webinars

Register for a free webinar to learn from Data Management experts on your favorite topics.

https://www.dataversity.net/category/education/webinars/upcoming-webinars/

DATAVERSITY Emails

Get the latest publications, news, and upcoming events. Receive emails specific to data topics, sign up for our e-newsletters, and be sure to stay up to date on all upcoming conferences.

https://content.dataversity.net/DVTC-DV-Subscribe_DVTC-DV-Subscribe.html

ADDITIONAL RESOURCES FROM ANTHONY ALGMIN

Algmin Data Leadership

Helping organizations of all kinds maximize their data value.
https://algmin.com/

Online Training

Data Leadership Learning Plan

In the Data Leadership Learning Plan, instructor Anthony Algmin examines how data professionals, and the enterprises they work for, can make the most of data.
https://training.dataversity.net/learning-paths/dl0-data-leadership-learning-plan

Data Modeling for Non-Data Professionals Learning Plan

The Data Modeling for Non-Data Professionals Learning Plan discusses the key concepts around Data Modeling and associated practices.

https://training.dataversity.net/learning-paths/
data-modeling-for-non-data-professionals-learning-plan

Data Governance for Non-Data Professionals Learning Plan

This Learning Plan is a collection of five different "What is…?" series of data fundamentals courses. It was developed to help data and non-data professionals build a common language and understanding between them on significant data-related topics.

https://training.dataversity.net/learning-paths/
data-governance-for-nondata-professionals-learning-plan

"What is…?" Build Your Own Bundle

These courses are meant to help data and non-data professionals build a common language and understanding between them on significant data-related topics such as Data Management, Data Governance, Data Stewardship, Data Modeling, Data Architecture, and many others.

https://training.dataversity.net/cart-collections/build-your-own-bundle

ABOUT THE AUTHOR

Anthony J. Algmin is the Founder of Algmin Data Leadership, a company helping business and technology leaders transform their future with data. With decades of experience in business and hands-on technology roles, Anthony brings better data management to organizations of all kinds. He has led data change initiatives in many industries, serving as a project manager, data architect, and Chief Data Officer.

A popular speaker and advocate for Data Leadership, Anthony makes frequent appearances at conferences and other events. He has a bachelor's degree from Illinois Wesleyan University and an MBA from the Kellogg School of Management. Anthony lives with his wife and three children in suburban Chicago.

INDEX

A

Agile, 151–155
Amazon Web Services, 103, 136
artificial intelligence, 101–104
automated data consumption mechanism, 92

B

back-end, 67
benchmarking, 18
big data, 135–136
blockchain, 96–97
breaches, 58–59
bridge-builder analogy, 38
business and IT divide. see IT and business divide
business glossary, 73
business metadata, 73
business perspective, 25
business process and operations, 122
business process automation, 104–105
business reality, management disconnect with, 124–125
business requirements, 21–22
business strategy, 109–110, 122
business-IT partnership, 22–23

C

CAO (Chief Analytics Officer), 126–129
CDO (Chief Data Officer), 126–129
    CIOs, 129
    CTOs, 129
    reporting structure, 128
    role and level of, 127
Chief Digital Officer. see CDO (Chief Data Officer)
CIOs, 129–130
CISO (Chief Information Security Officer), 28–29, 59–60
cloud, 95–96
    private, 140–142
    public, 136–140
communications, 21–22, 112–113

T

U